from survive to thrive

A Johns Hopkins Press
Health Book

from survive to thrive

Living Your Best Life with Mental Illness

Margaret S. Chisolm, MD
With John Hanc

Foreword by Cal Ripken Jr.
Illustrated by Natasha Chugh

 Johns Hopkins
University Press
Baltimore

Note to the Reader

This book is not meant to substitute for medical care, and treatment should not be based solely on its contents. Instead, treatment must be developed through a dialogue between the individual and his or her physician. The book has been written to help with that dialogue. The events described in this book are the real experiences of real people. However, the authors have altered many of their identities and, in some cases, created composite characters. Any resemblance between a character in this book and a real person therefore is entirely accidental.

© 2021 Johns Hopkins University Press
All rights reserved. Published 2021
Printed in the United States of America on acid-free paper
9 8 7 6 5 4 3 2 1

Johns Hopkins University Press
2715 North Charles Street
Baltimore, Maryland 21218-4363
www.press.jhu.edu

Library of Congress Cataloging-in-Publication Data
Names: Chisolm, Margaret S., author. | Hanc, John, author.
Title: From survive to thrive : living your best life with mental illness /
    Margaret S. Chisolm, MD, with John Hanc ; foreword by Cal Ripken Jr. ;
    illustrated by Natasha Chugh.
Description: Baltimore : Johns Hopkins University Press, 2021. | Series: A
    Johns Hopkins Press health book | Includes bibliographical references
    and index.
Identifiers: LCCN 2020045434 | ISBN 9781421441580 (hardcover) | ISBN
    9781421441603 (ebook)
Subjects: LCSH: Mental illness—Alternative treatment. | Psychotherapy. |
    Positive psychology. | Self-care, Health.
Classification: LCC RC480.5 .C48 2021 | DDC 616.89/14—dc23
LC record available at https://lccn.loc.gov/2020045434

A catalog record for this book is available from the British Library.

The questionnaire in chapter 1 is from T. J. VanderWeele, "On the Promotion of Human Flourishing," PNAS, 31:8148-56.

Special discounts are available for bulk purchases of this book. For more information, please contact Special Sales at specialsales@jh.edu.

To Michael

contents

foreword

Cal Ripken Jr.

When I was first asked to join the advisory council for the Paul McHugh Program for Human Flourishing, I had to ask the obvious question: What is flourishing? I knew the literal definition, but how was it going to be applied in helping others?

As a baseball player I did flourish. I had a dream to be a big league baseball player, and I worked very hard toward that goal. To say that things worked out would be an understatement. I was enshrined in the National Baseball Hall of Fame and won many awards, but that's not necessarily how I would define flourishing. Flourishing comes from within. It was my own personal sense of accomplishment, which was a source of pride, that helped bring meaning to my everyday life.

Accomplishment in your life, big or small, might be the secret to a life well lived. It gives us a sense of purpose, and we all want our lives to have meaning.

These accomplishments can come from any and all aspects of your life. Now, I was super focused on work (actually play—I had a fun job), but some of my most powerful feelings came out of my connections to my family and community. I had the great fortune of being teammates with my brother and my father. In fact, it was a first in Major League Baseball history to have a dad manage his two sons at the same time. So the experience was especially gratifying and fulfilling.

Billy, my brother, was my double play partner up the middle, as he played second base. The shortstop and the second baseman play a critical defensive role for a baseball team. We took that teamwork one step further, carrying it out at a higher level. Call it a better level of communication, or that we thought the same way, or that we were simply brothers and wanted to be the best. I thoroughly enjoyed that opportunity. It's the kind of enjoyment that sometimes we take for granted until it's gone.

There was no double play situation that Billy and I thought we couldn't complete. I remember working with Billy when the hitter and the base runner on first were both extremely fast runners. He asked where I needed the ball to come from for me to complete the double play. I showed him the exact spot, which he then called my holster. He showed me his holster spot, and we both knew that if we were able to hit the holster we could finish the play. I'm still trying to figure out that definition for flourishing, but I might have just found it with my brother Billy.

When I retired from baseball I was forty-one years old and got a bit lost trying to transition away from the game. I remembered one of my dad's favorite sayings, which helped my thinking at the time. He used to say that in order to be successful, you must learn to adjust and readjust. It applies in baseball and life as well.

Well, I adjusted to life without baseball, maybe by simply acknowledging that the world doesn't revolve around baseball. I readjusted by creating a foundation with my family to honor the legacy of my dad's life. It's called the Cal Ripken Sr. Foundation. We use baseball and the lessons of sports to give kids new opportunities to learn and grow. Many of the kids we serve face great challenges in their daily lives. To see them overcome family and peer issues, including major setbacks along the way, and succeed is so inspiring. To see these kids flourish gives me a much better sense of what the word means, for myself and especially for the kids.

Speaking of my dad, his dream of playing in the big leagues ended with an injury. He adjusted to being a coach and readjusted his life to one of teaching others to fulfill their dreams. One of his greatest skills was his ability to make you feel good about yourself. I call it filling your chest with air. When he gave us a task or chore like cleaning up our bedrooms or cutting the grass, he'd always take the time to look over our work. He'd say, "Look how good your room looks now . . . you did that . . . you should be proud." Or, "Look how straight your lines are in the grass, that's great work."

One of my favorite memories of chores relates to edging the driveway, which was definitely not my favorite chore. We were given two nail spikes, some string, and a hatchet. The spikes and the string were to help us create a straight line along the driveway. We used the hatchet to cut the grass on an angle. From the perspective of my brother and me, these were archaic tools. We were so jealous of our next door neighbor's electric edger. How could Dad really expect us to do a good job with these antiquated tools? Well, we did a great job, and he was thrilled with our work once he inspected it. He bragged about us to anyone who would listen. Teaching and being helpful to others was so meaningful to Dad. Now, that is flourishing all the way around.

I turned sixty last year, and I've found myself getting more philosophical with age. I ponder questions like, What is a good life? What's the meaning of your own life? What's a successful life? We all search for an answer. But I've learned that the answer may lie not in some great flash of philosophical insight but rather through what Dr. Chisolm identifies in this book as the four pathways to flourishing: family, work, education, and community. These are the components of a successful and meaningful life.

This book is particularly important because in addition to providing a road map for all of us, it offers hope for people with psychiatric illness (and their loved ones) that they too can flourish in life. By sharing her own story, Dr. Chisolm helps demystify and destigmatize psychiatric disorders. And drawing on her own and other cases, she outlines how anyone can reach their greatest potential. These four pathways are ones that have certainly been crucial in my own success.

I've learned a few lessons in my lifetime, and the beauty of life is that there are many more lessons for me to learn. I'll be looking for those opportunities to flourish and to enjoy the feeling that comes from the inside out.

from survive to thrive

Rise and Shine!

How This Book Can Help You Thrive

If you are seeing a health professional for a diagnosed mental illness, including addiction, this book is for you.

If you've visited a therapist to talk about the stresses of your job or issues with your family, this book is for you.

If your parent, child, or partner is battling mental health issues and you'd like to help your loved one lead a fuller, more satisfying life, this book is for you too.

And if your life is firing on all cylinders, if you are finding fulfillment at both home and work and you wake up each morning feeling cheerful and eager and whistle your way down the boulevard of life . . . well then, this book is *not* for you. Because, if you are that individual, you are one of a kind; the only person in the world who already has what we all want. And since that sounds like a perfect existence, we know it's probably not a realistic goal. Most of us are works in progress, all trying to get ever closer to that ideal—to get to a point where, to use the parlance of mental health professionals like myself, we are "flourishing."

I explore this term in more depth a little later in this book. But you don't need a definition to understand what I mean when I say that this is a book about how to lead a satisfying life, an optimal life. It is a book designed to help you take the steps needed to get to a place where you are happier, more productive, more at peace, and to take these steps no matter what conditions you may have or where you are in your life at present or how you may feel at this moment.

And if you *are* someone who is struggling, I have a pretty good sense of what that feeling is like.

I've been working with people experiencing various forms of mental illness for many years as a psychiatrist at Johns Hopkins University. My patients have battled, and in many cases overcome, everything from addiction and depression to bipolar disorder. I've seen some of my patients emerge from very dark places and then, as if by magic, soar. To the point where they are today leading the kind of fulfilled, satisfying life many people only dream about.

Of course, it wasn't magic. It was the application of various forms of treatments and interventions as well as their diligence and desire to get better that helped them. In many cases, they followed the same principles and adopted some of the same approaches that I recommend in this book.

There's one more reason that I can relate to those who are confronting mental health disorders. In my own life, I too have battled them, as have members of my family.

I'll share my story later in this book. But first, let's talk about your story and about the ideas and approaches that can help you change the narrative of your own life.

A note about exactly who "you" are: this book is for a person struggling with mental illness or despair. But you may be reading this on behalf of a loved one rather than for yourself. If that is the case, rest assured that you will find support and guidance here. But this book is also directed to anyone who wants to lead a better life. So, even if you've been fortunate enough not to have dealt with mental illness, you can still use some of the approaches in this book to make your life better. You can still gain useful insights into your own sense of well-being or discover new strategies for self-improvement.

The Four Perspectives

In the next chapter of this book, I fully define our goal—the achievement of this exalted-sounding state of "flourishing," which essentially is when we reach our greatest potential.

How do you get there? The first step is by better understanding where you are now and what the underlying causes of your mental illness may be. Some of the causes might seem clear to you; some you may have discovered (or will discover) in therapy. Regardless, before we can transition toward a more fulfilled life, we have to better understand why we're not fulfilled now.

What's holding you back—and why?

The answer to that question isn't always obvious. Unlike in the case of other illnesses, there are often multiple explanations for what causes the conditions I treat. With a knee injury suffered by a football player who gets caught in a pile-up at the line of scrimmage, or a cough and cold that a person who works in a day care center with young children develops, the cause is straightforward. There is usually no clear, definite answer to the question of what caused a mental illness.

Nor is there a gold standard test—no X-ray, MRI, or throat swab—for diagnosing these disorders. In almost all cases, a health professional's examination and communication skills are crucial—their ability to ask the right questions in the right way and listen to your responses is critical to their making the right diagnosis.

Your illness could have been primarily provoked by things you've encountered or endured in your life. Or it might be mostly because of the type of person you are; you may be someone whose emotions change quickly or who isn't particularly flexible. Or your illness could be linked mainly to something you're doing—using or overusing certain substances; restricting food intake; repeating some counterproductive behavior pattern. Or just as with certain physical illnesses, your mental illness could be primarily due to a broken part or function (and not only in the brain).

Although sometimes a mental illness only has one explanation, given that these illnesses occur in the context of real human beings who have unique stories and personalities, there is usually more than one explanation. So it makes sense that no one approach, method, or perspective can provide the clarity we need to help treat that illness most effectively. So mental health professionals have developed four lenses through which we attempt to discern what may be causing the problem, whether it's addiction, depression, bipolar disorder, or simply the blues.

The first is the **life story perspective**, which recognizes the importance of events in a person's life that may be relevant to their current mental illness; the second is the **dimensional perspective**, which takes into account the cognitive and temperamental aspects of a person in understanding their current mental distress; the third is the **behavior perspective**, which considers patterns in a person's behavior that arise from conditioned learning; the fourth is the **disease perspective**, which understands mental illness as arising from a broken part or function, often—but not always—originating in the brain.

The following images sum up the four perspectives:

the frog reading a book icon for the life story perspective reminds us of the importance of the personal narrative in mental illness

the folded piece of paper for the dimensional perspective represents the way various personality dimensions can—if extreme—lead to mental distress

the rat in the cage for the behavior perspective suggests how a person can find themselves stuck in certain behavior patterns

the bear with the broken arm for the disease perspective reflects the idea of the broken part or function inherent to this perspective

As we explore each of these, chapter by chapter, you'll get a better understanding of each of these factors and, more importantly, of how they apply in your situation. For now, think of the four perspectives in simpler terms, through the acronym HIDE. It means that every case, every person, can be seen in four different ways. They might be someone who

Has a condition or mental illness of some sort.
You've been diagnosed with clinical depression, bipolar disorder, or dementia.

Is a certain way (that is, has a certain type of personality).
You are gregarious or shy; you are low key or hot tempered.

Does something (that is, behaves in a particular way).
You're overeating or deliberately avoiding food. You're drinking more than you should or you're cutting or harming yourself to cope.

Encounters specific circumstances in life that contribute to
their illness.
You've suffered the loss of a loved one or gone through a divorce.
You've lost a job or witnessed a traumatic event.

I delve into these perspectives in the chapters that follow and explain
them in greater depth, including the concepts and mechanisms underlying each. In each chapter, I also share with you detailed case studies
from my own practice that illustrate these perspectives. Identities are
disguised, of course, to protect privacy, but they are all based on real
people I've worked with (and a few that I haven't, but whose names you
may recognize).

In addition, I offer some insights, tips, and takeaways from each of the
case studies that you can then apply to your own situation. And finally,
a self-assessment is provided that you can use to better understand the
way each of these perspectives has affected your own life.

One last point about the HIDE acronym: it reminds us that mental
disorders are often publicly *hidden* in addition to being complex and elu-
sive in their presentation.

Road Map for Flourishing: The Four Pathways

The four perspectives can help us understand what's holding us back, which in turn can often enable us to move forward.

After exploring the four perspectives, we'll consider four other variables in the flourishing equation. Just as there are our distinct lenses through which a person's mental status can be viewed for the purpose of individualized diagnosis and treatment, there are (coincidentally) four particular categories of life experience that we can identify as pathways toward achieving a richer, more meaningful existence:

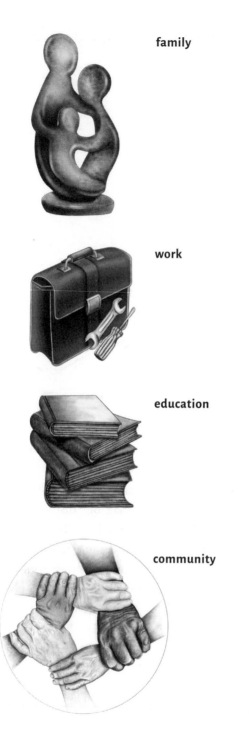

family

work

education

community

Think of these as building blocks to a successful life. And when they're not fully constructed or when they've been damaged by our behaviors or other factors in our past, they keep us from moving forward.

I see this frequently with my patients who are battling addiction. They're not working up to their potential. They don't have real friends outside of the people they use with. They aren't connected to any kind of stable community. They're aimlessly trying to fumble through a bad situation, one day at a time.

Even if you're not battling an addiction, you may feel the same way —as if you've taken a wrong exit off the road that was your life, and now you're lost. In these kinds of situations, you need to get back on the right road, the one leading toward a better life. Getting a reliable map so that they can get back on that route is what I help my patients with—and I can help you as well.

I'm sure the importance of these aspects of life has been stressed to you in the past. Maybe to a point where the insistence on their significance has come to seem like a cliché to you. But before you roll your eyes or dismiss them out of hand because of negative experiences with your parents, a boss, a teacher, or a priest or minister, understand that I take a broader view of each of these concepts. For instance, family might not just mean your family of origin, but the family of lifelong friends you create for yourself. These pathways, which may seem blocked or inaccessible to you now, can be navigated in a slightly different way than before to get you where you want to be.

The chapters of this book that focus on these pathways aim to put you back in the driver's seat of your life and provide you with a road map to follow. To give you a better sense of the process, let's consider just one of the pathways here, briefly: work.

Allow me to extend the driving metaphor here a bit. One way of looking at the process of flourishing is as a road, with the destination being satisfaction, happiness, and financial security. Certainly, there are people who extol the virtues of shedding material things in life or living with nothing. The reality is, however, that most of us need to work to put a roof over our heads and bread on the table.

Beyond the monetary rewards, work can help you thrive and flourish because it can offer a sense of meaning and purpose to your life. Study after study has shown that work is good for your health. This is one reason older folks are often urged not to retire completely. Research has shown that those who retire at relatively early ages have greater health problems than their peers who continue in some form of employment.

Those who work accrue other benefits. Let's consider again the example of those battling drug addiction.

For those with substance use disorders, if they are willing and able to work, a job gives them a reason to get up in the morning. In and of itself, a job provides structure in a life that, up to this point, has likely been based around buying and using drugs. People who are trying to overcome their problematic use of substances and who are employed interact and form relationships with people whose lives do not revolve around drug use: their coworkers. A job gives them a purpose, an accountability, regardless of how inherently rewarding or challenging the job is. When you have a job, somebody's expecting you to show up; someone has charged you with a responsibility. That can itself lead to a subtle but powerful shift in one's mindset.

Ask any military recruiter about the power of that connectedness. The reason an eighteen-year-old joins the Marines, for example, is not likely just because they offer free housing or a good retirement package. It's also probably because they want to feel part of something bigger than themselves. Granted, not all jobs offer the prestige of being a Marine, but someone is still depending on you to do something, even if it's pushing a broom or working in a fast-food restaurant, and thus you are connected to something bigger.

Getting back to the disease of addiction, the research is instructive. There are studies going on at Johns Hopkins about how to deter this destructive force. One of them strikes me as quite promising. The idea is that as opposed to paying people *not* to use drugs—an effective but not-very-popular way of fighting addiction—we instead look at the effect of allowing people to work and earn pay so long as they are not using. In this scenario, a person recovering from addiction must give a urine sample before they are given the opportunity to earn their pay. They show up at the workplace and get tested on the spot. If no drug use is detected, they're allowed to work.

The results of this approach so far are encouraging. What those results tell me is that as much as we may grouse about our jobs on a day-to-day basis, people want to work. Perhaps we instinctively realize that doing some kind of regular activity gives our lives cohesion and structure as well as purpose. You need not work forty hours a week in a factory or an office or even bring home a paycheck to get the benefits of employment. There are some people who, for various reasons, can't work a conventional job. But in the digital age, and especially in the wake of the 2020 coronavirus epidemic and the workplace changes that resulted from the quarantine, it's more possible than ever to participate in some kind of paid or unpaid job—an endeavor that assigns you responsibilities, that sets expectations for your behavior, and that yields appreciation in one form or another for your efforts.

This pathway can be pursued through volunteer work (which is what some of my patients battling depression have done, with excellent results). There are organizations that need your help, no matter how unhelpful you may presently feel. Remember, there's always somebody worse off than you, and that somebody—or a group or charity that represents them—would welcome your assistance.

I'm thinking about a patient of mine, Jessica, who had agoraphobia—a type of anxiety disorder that makes you fear places you believe could cause you to panic and make you feel trapped or helpless. Very often, the person with this disorder is afraid to leave their home.

Jessica, who was terribly afraid of crowds, rarely ventured out of her house. Because animals have been shown to help reduce the feelings of panic and anxiety associated with agoraphobia, she was encouraged to get a dog. She fell in love with her faithful golden lab Brandy. Having Brandy around turned out to be so beneficial to Jessica that she decided to apply for a job training companion animals for others, which she got. This new responsibility required her to go out into large crowds with the animals she was training, something that would have triggered panic attacks in the past. But with a dog by her side, she was able to do it.

Jessica continues in her job training service animals, and she has since begun to reengage with the wider world. She's a much happier and more confident young lady. I think you could say she is thriving, and work was one of the pathways that enabled her to achieve that goal.

What to Expect from This Book

Perhaps you are asking yourself whether it really is possible to flourish and lead a fulfilling life with a mental illness. The answer is a resounding yes, and this book will tell you how. What I've written in these pages is based on years of experience with rigorous attention to evidence-based research and treatment outcomes, both at Johns Hopkins and, before that, in private practice. I share what I have learned and describe my experiences in the spirit of optimism and in the sincere belief that those suffering from psychiatric conditions do indeed have the potential to lead healthier and more fulfilling lives.

My experience with my patients over the years has shown me that people with mental health challenges are capable of making vast improvements and can go on to build or resume lives that are happy and fulfilling in every sense. But my experience with my patients also compels me to offer an important caveat here: unlike a book that shows you how to grow a vegetable garden or develop a muscular core, the book is not, and cannot be, a one-size-fits-all approach.

Some people with psychiatric illnesses can, with the help of intensive therapy and the right medications, feel better and pick up their lives where they left off. For example, if you start using substances as an adolescent, any addiction that develops can certainly interrupt your life's trajectory and worse, but in part because you're still young, you can (with proper treatment) usually bounce back and lead a full life. But other forms of mental illness—psychosis, schizophrenia, or bipolar disorder—are often diagnosed in adulthood, when many of the structures of your life are fully established. When your mental health goes awry, those structures—family, friends, career—may be damaged to such an extent that it would be hard to regain the trajectory you once were on.

For that reason, I don't want to say "read this book and you can get back to the person you once were!" The person you used to be might not be the person you now wish to be. Further, the reality is that a mental illness may be severe enough that it will permanently alter the arc of your life. Even then, however, it's a matter of forging new pathways, building new community structures or family relationships, or, as we just discussed, finding new forms of work.

My approach to flourishing—helping a person understand the four perspectives and then helping them set out to navigate the four pathways—is not meant to be the same for everyone. The variables in your

HIDE profile will be different than someone else's, as will be the way you navigate those pathways.

Variables in the treatment you are currently receiving will also play a role in how this books works for you. For example, perhaps you are seeing a therapist regularly at the time you're reading this book. You might also be taking antidepressant medication. Or it could be that you're not seeing a therapist regularly but you are getting a script reapproved for your meds once a year. Regardless of where you are in your treatment, this book can help. It might help you become more open to treatment and to understand better what we mental health professionals are trying to accomplish in our sessions. It might raise questions you want to ask your therapist or stimulate ideas you want to share with them; that is, ideas for actions you can take that can help you to flourish.

Yes, *action*. People often seem to think that therapy consists of only talking about your feelings, followed by *more* talking about your feelings. But often the most successful therapeutic interventions are based on helping patients focus on goals—and taking steps toward those goals.

Which is precisely what I hope you will be able to do after reading this book. So, by all means, if you're getting professional help, use this book as a supplement. It might make the whole process even more beneficial. But regardless of where you are now, and regardless of the route you will take, this book is indeed for you.

In other words, no matter how dark it may seem now, you can reach a point in your life where you can flourish. What exactly that destination looks like and how to know when you've arrived is the subject of the next chapter.

chapter 1

Are You Flourishing?

Defining What It Means to Thrive

A bold or extravagant gesture.

A musical fanfare of trumpets.

A distinctive, ornamental curve in handwriting.

The word "flourish" has many meanings: according to the *Oxford English Dictionary*, its lineage is as complex as the roots of a plant—appropriately so, as the word is derived from the Old French "floriss," which in turn is based on the Latin *florere*, from *flos* or *flor*.

Meaning "flower."

While the term has been used in many ways, it is the definition of it as "to grow or develop in a healthy or vigorous way"—or, to harken back to the literal definition, "to flower"—that I am interested in here.

Charles Dickens used the word in this sense to describe the verdant English countryside in midsummer, in a beautiful passage from *Oliver Twist*: "The earth had donned her mantle of brightest green; and shed her richest perfumes abroad. It was the prime and vigour of the year; all things were glad and flourishing."

Although we might tend to associate flourishing, with its connotations of robust growth, with commerce, it has also been associated with a question that great minds have been asking for centuries, namely, what is human happiness? In his *Nicomachean Ethics*, Aristotle uses the word *eudaimonia* to consider this question, for which "human flourishing" has been proposed as the most accurate translation. It means "to grow" or "to prosper"—indeed, the very definition of flourishing.

In his 2017 *The Sermon on the Mount and Human Flourishing*, theologian Jonathan Pennington eloquently notes that "human flourishing has been and is the driving force behind every philosophy and religion known to humanity." "Whether it is Stoicism, Epicureanism, Islam, Platonism, new atheism, Christianity, the ancient worship of Baal and Asherah, Joel Osteen's *Your Best Life Now*, Buddhism, Positive Psychology, the Beachbody exercise company, or Judaism, the bedrock motivation and *telos* (end goal) for all humanity is for life, and life more abundant."

Those of us in the field of mental health have likewise embraced—whether we're aware of it or not—the notion of flourishing. Martin Seligman, a leader in positive psychology, helped popularize the term in the world of self-improvement. Seligman's PERMA model of flourishing (**p**ositive emotions, **e**ngagement, **r**elationships, **m**eaning, **a**chievements) has led to major advances in the study of psychological well-being. It does not, however, address physical health or aspects of character and virtue, and many philosophers have argued that being a good person is part of leading a good life. Under this definition, a dictator or drug lord who has accumulated great power or material wealth but who has done so on the backs of his people or through cold-blooded crimes might be prosperous—but he is certainly not flourishing.

Here at Johns Hopkins, following the example of the founder of our Psychiatry Department, Adolf Meyer, the members of the department have consistently acted on a core belief that mental health is not simply the lack of mental illness. We have long been a leader in humanistic clinical practice, incorporating Meyer's emphasis on the well-being of the whole person into the way in which we systematically assess and treat people with mental health problems. We do this by applying the perspectives approach I described in the introduction and that I elaborate on in the next few chapters.

This approach toward treating the whole person led us to seek a more all-encompassing definition of flourishing. My colleagues and I at Hopkins are now collaborating with Harvard University epidemiologist Tyler J. VanderWeele, who has identified four pathways that lead to happiness and health, which you will recognize as the four pathways to flourishing that I have also outlined in the introduction:

family

work

education

community

Again, I hasten to add, there are many trajectories on each of these pathways, such as getting married or staying single with respect to the family pathway, or finding a paying job or volunteering with respect to the work pathway. Each of the four pathways are important parts of life, and feeling satisfied with each demands long-term effort (we all know the old saying "nothing worth having comes easily"). Success in each requires a demonstration of personal responsibility. And all are aspects of life that you can change or alter, create or remake. In other words, no matter where you are now, there are things you can do, steps you can take to make yourself happier, to flourish.

You'll notice that I've used the terms "happiness" and "flourishing" as if they were synonymous. While they are close, there are differences. Dr. VanderWeele argues that flourishing is "a state in which all aspects of a person's life are good," a state in which one is not just happy but has achieved health in its fullest sense. In a 2019 article in the *Journal of the American Medical Association*, he outlines a "flourishing index" that identifies six key domains of happiness and health: happiness and life satisfaction, physical and mental health, meaning and purpose, character and virtue, close social relationships, and financial and material security.

To flourish, though, one does not have to be absolutely satisfied in every one of these areas. Few of us can achieve that. But this comprehensive list does give a sense of the many facets of what it means to truly flourish.

Although Dr. VanderWeele identifies mental health as one aspect of flourishing, it is not a prerequisite to success. In fact, we know that psychological struggles can promote growth. Psychologists Richard Tedeschi and Lawrence Calhoun have shown that people who struggle after experiencing traumatic events often demonstrate positive psychological growth later. They call this phenomenon "posttraumatic growth," for which concentration camp survivor and psychiatrist Victor Frankl may be the prime example. In his book *Man's Search for Meaning*, Frankl describes how humans have an innate drive to find meaning in their lives. It is this drive that he credits in helping him endure and overcome the trauma of the Holocaust.

But even less extreme experiences can be enlightening and promote positive growth. From these events, Tedeschi explains, "people develop new understandings of themselves, the world they live in, how to relate to other people, the kind of future they might have and a better understanding of how to live life."

In other words, you can still flourish even if you are struggling psychologically, have been diagnosed with a mental illness, or are experiencing adverse life events. This is one of the underlying principles of this book. I believe it wholeheartedly because I have seen it with my own eyes with patients who have come from highly dysfunctional families, have faced very challenging situations, have a serious disease, or have made very poor choices (again, think of those four perspectives). Yet they have managed to flourish.

You can, too.

Case Study

Paul, now in his late thir-
ties, grew up in the suburbs of
Philadelphia, the son of an engi-
neer and a teacher. His childhood
seemed a relatively happy one.
He was an outstanding student;
his parents had high hopes that

he'd graduate college and maybe even go on to a profession. But during
high school, he began to exhibit troubling signs. He started talking to
voices no one else heard and worried that his closest friends were now
trying to harm him. Paul was eventually diagnosed with schizophrenia,
a serious form of mental illness. It was made worse by drug use: while
Paul was in college, he experimented and found that even relatively mod-
erate use of alcohol or marijuana had extremely negative effects on him.

He eventually dropped out of school and went on a downward spiral.
A few months later, Paul was hospitalized for the first time—against his
wishes. This may have been the appropriate course of action for him at
that point, but was of course, deeply disturbing to him, as well as to his
parents—who had tried very hard to support him.

During the first few years of his illness, Paul continued to do poorly
and was hospitalized many times. His hallucinations and delusions per-
sisted, and for a while it seemed that he might never get better. But when
new antipsychotic drugs became available, things changed dramatically
for Paul.

Thanks to these new medications, his symptoms improved markedly.
He was soon discharged, and I saw him a week later and then periodically afterward. It was about a year after his discharge from that hospitalization that I really noticed the biggest changes, starting with his personal appearance. Paul arrived in my office that day clean shaven, with
his hair trimmed and wearing neatly pressed khaki pants and a stylish
dress shirt. He gave me a smile as he entered my office, a contrast to the

scowl with which he'd greeted me at most of his past visits. During those sessions, Paul also sported a scraggly, unkempt beard and had been wearing sweat clothes. He didn't seem back then to be someone who cared about his appearance. Clearly, that had changed.

Here's part of the conversation we had that day in my office (and of course, the specifics about this patient and our interaction have been changed to protect privacy):

Dr. Chisolm: It's good to see you looking so well.

Paul: Thanks, doctor. I feel pretty good. Actually, very good.

Dr. C.: "Very" good? I like to hear that! What's going on?

Paul: Well, I've stayed out of the hospital, as you know, and I've been doing great in the group home, but the big news is that I now have my own apartment. Nothing fancy . . . a one bedroom above a garage near my parents . . . but it's pretty nice.

Dr. C.: That's wonderful news! What do you think is the reason you're doing so well?

Paul: Well, I've stayed on my medication, for one. And it's working. I haven't had any episodes since then.

Dr. C.: And any voices or worries that anyone is trying to harm you?

Paul: No. I hope that's all behind me now. I think it will be if I stick with these meds, right?

Dr. C.: Sounds like that's what has helped you the most. But I'm curious: what are you doing with your time?

Paul: Well, recently, I've been pretty busy with the apartment. I had a lot of help. My mom and my girlfriend went shopping with me to pick out stuff . . . you know, wallpaper and rugs and all that . . . and they made it look really nice. Really homey.

Dr. C.: Wait. Girlfriend?

Paul: Yeah. Cathy. She's really cool. I met her a while back at this volunteer gig I've been doing, but we've been hanging out a lot more in the last month or so.

Dr. C.: You mentioned last time that you were doing some volunteer work. Tell me more about that—and about her.

Paul: I started volunteering a couple days a week at the clinic I used to go to. It's kind of grunt work really. They need me to move boxes around or sit and talk with someone if they're having a bad day. I do whatever they need.

Dr. C.: I'm sure that what you're doing is valuable to them. And you met Cathy there?

Paul: Yeah, she's like an administrative assistant at the clinic. So, she has no problem with me and where I've been. She's even met my family.

Dr. C.: And how have they been?

Paul: Fine. My one nephew—Jason—just had a birthday. He's sixteen now. His brother is still a little kid.

Dr. C.: Do you have a relationship with them?

Paul: Oh, sure. My brother always has everyone over on the holidays. Jason likes to talk to me. He knows I'm not going to get on his case like his dad does [laughs]. We talk about working out, about school, whatever.

Dr. C.: Do you belong to a gym?

Paul: Yup. Hey, I gotta stay in shape to lift those boxes around, right? I go a few times a week, mainly weights and the treadmill. It makes me feel good.

Dr. C.: That's great. You've found out yourself what the research has shown: that exercise is helpful for managing anxiety and reducing stress. Let me ask you a question about your nephew Jason. Do you think he knows about what you've been through?

Paul: You mean back in the day? Good question. I'm sure at some point my brother or sister-in-law had to explain why Uncle Paulie wasn't around for all those years. But he never brings it up.

Dr. C.: And if he or his brother did ask about your illness, would you have a problem talking about it?

Paul: I don't think so. In fact, I talked about it at the clinic. One guy . . . a teenager, he was kind of strung out, I was with him one night while they were making calls to social services . . . he was telling me how messed up his life was. I said, "Dude, no offense, but you don't know messed up." And I kind of told him a little about what I'd been through. He looked at me like I had two heads. "No way," he said. "You seem like so normal. I would never have thought you were nuts!" [laughs].

Dr. C.: That's not a very nice way to put it.

Paul: I thought it was funny. And it was kind of a compliment. Hey, he was a kid, having a bad time. Maybe I helped him a little bit that night.

Dr. C.: I'm sure you did. How is it being back in your old neighborhood?

Paul: It's good to be near my folks. Sometimes it's a little weird, though, to see people. I was in the store the other day, picking up a few things for dinner. Cathy was coming over. I ran into this guy from high school. "Do I know you?" he asked. "Yeah," I said, "It's Paul." He was shocked. "I thought you were . . . er . . . away." He didn't know what to say. "I was," I told him. "But I'm doing fine now." But I guess not as fine as him. I saw him pull out of the parking lot later in a Benz.

Dr. C.: People often don't know what to say, you're right. OK, so you're living independently, you're volunteering at the clinic, you've got a girlfriend, you're going to the gym. Anything else?

Paul: Yeah, well I'm thinking about taking classes in the fall. Finally going back to school. Part time at first. I'll be like the oldest one in my class.

Dr. C.: What are you thinking about studying?

Paul: Psychology. Maybe I could do a research paper on the abnormal brain and write about myself!

Dr. C.: Oh, come on.

Paul: I'm just kidding. But I did meet with the professor who teaches Psych 101. She happened to be in her office the day I went over to find out about registering. She was pretty cool. She's a therapist and just teaches part time. I talked with her a little bit about my background.

Dr. C.: That's interesting. What did she say?

Paul: She's heard about the medications I take, and I told her a little bit about where I've been. And she said, "Hey, you're doing great."
Dr. C.: You know what? I agree with your professor!

Paul's story is inspiring on many levels. I can tell you that schizophrenia is a serious mental illness. And for the parents, it must have seemed like a death sentence to commit their young adult child to a psychiatric hospital. They must have felt as if they would never see their son again, and that he'd be lost for the rest of his life in this dark fog.

But he's turned it around. Now let's be clear: Paul's story is unusual in the speed with which he was able to make changes. Normally, I would expect the things that Paul was able to do to occur over a decades-long time period.

Still, he reminds us what's possible.

A lot of people get credit here, including his parents and the professionals he worked with at the hospital, not to mention the pharmaceutical researchers who developed the drugs that turned his life around. We hear a lot about the negative effects of many prescription medicines; this one, I would submit, has been a life-changing positive for many.

Ultimately, though, it was Paul himself who took control of his life and steered it on a new course. He's leading as normal a life as possible, and because he's still a young man, there is much to look forward to, and there are even more improvements that can be made.

The message here is that you can live a full life, you really can, even if doing so means adjusting your expectations. I could tell that Paul felt a little bit of that "if only" feeling when he talked about meeting his old classmate who was apparently materially successful. I think part of him thinks "I could have been driving a Mercedes Benz now, too, if it wasn't for my illness." That's something he'll have to get over. If he wanted to pursue a degree, could he eventually become a college graduate? Could he find a career direction and a high-salaried job? Certainly, but Paul's illness was severe, and it is something that will have to be closely monitored and treated the rest of his life.

The point is that it's often not helpful to compare yourself to your peers and where they are. Depending on your age and situation, who knows? You may eventually surpass some of them. You may be a late bloomer. Regardless, you can lead a full life. A life, as Dr. VanderWeele would say, in which all aspects are good.

That's Paul's life. And by any definition, it's a good one—especially relative to where he's been. In my mind, there's no doubt about it.

Paul is flourishing.

How about you? Where are you at in your life? Let's find out.

Self-Reflection

Dr. VanderWeele developed this questionnaire to help measure the extent to which you are flourishing. Please respond to the following questions on a scale from 0 to 10:

Overall, how satisfied are you with life as a whole these days?

0 = not satisfied at all, 10 = completely satisfied _____

In general, how happy or unhappy do you usually feel?

0 = extremely unhappy, 10 = extremely happy _____

In general, how would you rate your physical health?

0 = poor, 10 = excellent _____

How would you rate your overall mental health?

0 = poor, 10 = excellent   _____

Overall, to what extent do you feel the things you do in your life are worthwhile?

0 = not at all worthwhile, 10 = completely worthwhile   _____

I understand my purpose in life.

0 = strongly disagree, 10 = strongly agree   _____

I always act to promote good in all circumstances, even in difficult and challenging situations.

0 = not true of me, 10 = completely true of me   _____

I am always able to give up some happiness now for greater happiness later.

0 = not true of me, 10 = completely true of me   _____

I am content with my friendships and relationships.

0 = strongly disagree, 10 = strongly agree   _____

My relationships are as satisfying as I would want them to be.

0 = strongly disagree, 10 = strongly agree   _____

How often do you worry about being able to meet normal monthly living expenses?

0 = worry all of the time, 10 = do not ever worry   _____

How often do you worry about safety, food, or housing?

0 = worry all of the time, 10 = do not ever worry   _____

Now total up your score, and divide by 12.

Flourishing Index Score   _____

If your score is less than 6, this book has much to offer you. Regardless of your score, chances are there are things you can do to improve your state of well-being. That's the goal here: to help you grow, improve—that is, flourish.

chapter 2

A New Vision for Understanding Mental Illness

In the previous chapter, we learned about the concept of flourishing and its relevance to mental well-being and happiness. But if you've been diagnosed with a mental illness, the last thing you might be thinking about is all the ways you might go about leading a full life. You want relief from your distress, plain and simple. You want to feel less stressed and anxious. That's understandable: when you feel pain—whether in your body or your mind—you go into survival mode. You just want to get through today. Achieving flourishing as defined by my colleague Dr. VanderWeele—"a state in which all aspects of a person's life are good"— may seem like a pipe dream. All aspects of life good? How can anything be good when you can barely drag yourself out of bed, when you're battling a craving for alcohol or drugs, or when you can't shut off the noise in your head?

I understand that feeling, but while it may seem a long-term if not impossible goal, the truth is that you can reach that state. It may take time and effort, but it's doable. People with mental illness thrive and flourish and have been doing so for centuries.

Dr. Martin Luther King, for example, struggled with depression and suicidal ideation. But like so many others, he was not simply defined by his mental challenges. He confronted them while at the same time battling segregation and racism and becoming the brilliant leader of the civil rights movement that we today memorialize in a national holiday. It is clear that Dr. King, one of the most important figures in American history, flourished, despite his short life. But he flourished *while* dealing with mental illness.

While few have attained his stature or greatness, there are other luminaries with similar profiles. In her memoir *An Unquiet Mind*, my Johns Hopkins colleague Dr. Kay Jamison recounts her experiences with manic-depressive illness and how she juggled a hectic and productive academic life while managing her illness. And in *The Center Cannot Hold*, Elyn Saks describes how she is able to lead a full life, despite having schizophrenia.

Certain mental illnesses have been linked with creativity, as Dr. Jamison points out in her book *Touched with Fire: Manic-Depressive Illness and the Artistic Temperament* and explores more deeply in the Pulitzer Prize–nominated biography *Robert Lowell, Setting the River on Fire: A Study of Genius, Mania, and Character*.

Of course, that great American poet was not the only creative luminary with mental illness. Biographers of Vincent van Gogh, Franz Kafka, Sylvia Plath, Ernest Hemingway, and many others remind us that with artistic genius often comes mental distress.

The works of these artists and others make it evident that we humans have a special gift. Not only are we able to feel and think, but—unique among species—we are able to reflect creatively on our feelings and thoughts and on the consequences of our actions. As we grow and develop, we start to notice patterns in how we typically feel, think, act, and react in all sorts of situations. In time, we become curious as to why we behave in these characteristic ways, especially when, as often happens, these habits result in unhappiness and frustration.

With maturity, most of us come to see that it is possible to break out of these typical patterns and so feel better mentally and even physically. If the way we feel and think gradually changes for the worse, we may or may not notice. If the changes happen more suddenly, we may notice them but explain them away. But those around us often have a better perspective. A deviation from what has been normal behavior can be deeply concerning for our friends and family and very difficult for them to understand. Just as perplexing can be someone who *never* feels, thinks, or acts in ways that seem appropriate. How do we make sense of these deviations from what is considered normal?

Understanding the basics of mental well-being—and how it can be compromised—is a critical step to helping people with mental illness flourish. At Johns Hopkins, we take a certain approach to mental illness known as the "perspectives of psychiatry." This view holds that not unlike plants and animals, some psychiatric disorders cluster into "families" or "kinds," based on their origins rather than their appearance, and that a goal of contemporary psychiatry should be to have such a classification system (just as every other science-based endeavor does).

This approach to thinking about mental well-being and illness has been the foundation for the training of many generations of Hopkins psychiatrists. These psychiatrists have, in turn, shared these ideas with their students as well as with their individual patients both here at Hopkins and around the world.

Although we have readings we share with our students on this topic, this is the first book geared specifically to patients and their families. I am excited to be able to share this approach, which I often call the "whole person framework" because that captures its essence.

While this isn't a textbook on psychiatry, if you have been dealing with a mental illness, it's probably useful to review some of the other approaches, some of which your therapist or clinician may have used with you.

The American Psychiatric Association's *Diagnostic and Statistical Manual of Mental Disorders*, often referred to as the "bible" of psychiatry, is well known. Less familiar may be internal medicine doctor George Engel's biopsychosocial model. Both of these provide the basis for psychiatry's current approach to mental illness. The *DSM* details distinct categories of psychiatric conditions, based on a patient's signs and symptoms, allowing scientists to study groups of patients with similar symptoms, which in turn has led to limited advancements in prognosis and treatment. The *DSM* also provides a common language for psychiatrists to describe a collection of symptoms displayed by a patient and "assign" a diagnosis to the patient.

That's a good thing. However, over time, psychiatrists have come to use the appearance-driven *DSM* in the same way a naturalist uses a field guide to identify birds or trees. You see a certain type of bill or coloring or leaf, and that's a clue that as to the species. But while that is a useful approach to identifying birds, it is not necessarily a good way to identify or understand mental illness. People with mental health conditions cannot be reduced to diseased brains or imbalanced chemical profiles; rather they are individuals whose unique life story and personality are paramount in understanding their challenges.

The biopsychosocial model offers an alternative way of understanding mental life. It simply reminds clinicians to consider the multiple and complex aspects of individuals—from the subatomic particles that make them up to the biosphere in which they live. It provides the list of ingredients relevant to all medical diagnosis, modified for psychiatry, but offers no recipe for applying these to the care of patients.

By contrast, the perspectives model presents a commonsense approach to understanding our feelings, thoughts, and actions in both states of mental well-being and mental illness. In using this approach, we view each person holistically and systematically from four different perspectives, which allows us to begin to understand the origins of their mental life.

The Hopkins approach uses the visual metaphor of looking at a person from different points of view, or perspectives, to describe how the feelings, thoughts, and actions that characterize mental well-being are shaped by a person's life story, by dimensions of personality, by behavior patterns, and by mental health understood as a matter of brain and body health and to account for how these feelings, thoughts, and actions can go awry in mental illness. In the rest of this chapter, I present the central concepts of each of these four perspectives—the life story, dimensional, behavior, and disease perspectives—and then in subsequent chapters devoted to each perspective, I explore each in more detail using case studies and histories to guide the way.

The Life Story Perspective

Each of us has a uniquely personal life story. Our lives unfold in a series of circumstances and events that may be similar to but are nonetheless distinct from anyone else's. We go through life as free agents with our own personal needs, desires, goals, hopes, and dreams. When all is going well, we feel that we are captain of our ship, in control of our life, and we work toward goals such as attaining wealth or security, finding the ideal mate, or creating the perfect family as we envision it.

But like most captains, we eventually hit turbulence: life circumstances that disrupt our hopes and dreams and throw us off course, leaving us distressed and demoralized. We have the sense of losing mastery over our life. This feeling can be temporary or sustained, but it does not usually result in serious mental illness. Almost all of us experience such demoralization at some point in life, and we are usually able to bounce back without much trouble. If we cannot rebound on our own, we might see a clinician for help in getting our life back on track, for help in changing the narrative of that life story, so to speak.

Grief is another emotion that is a part of just about everyone's life story. After the loss of a loved one, for instance, most of us have a predictable experience: emotional numbness, followed by disbelief and recurrent memories of the deceased. These feelings and thoughts are usually accompanied by periods or outpourings of sadness and crying ("wellings" is what we call these in psychiatry). Our sleep, appetite, and daily activities may also change. Over time, these feelings slowly resolve and move into the background of our mind, especially with the support of others and the resumption of our normal daily activities. Our morale is restored and life eventually goes on. (There can always be a lingering emotional wound such that even years later, a memory of our late loved one might trigger a brief "welling" spell.)

Although grief is a normal human reaction to loss, some of us may choose to seek professional support to help to deal with our experience of it. But grieving, even intensely and over a long period of time, is not a mental illness.

The life story perspective emphasizes that our mental well-being, or at least some aspect of it, arises from our psychological reactions to life events, such as a personal loss or other stressful circumstances. The essential feature of this perspective is that we can explain, in a meaningful way, our reaction to this event, how we are feeling, thinking, or acting in response to the situation.

Normally, our reaction is proportionate in content and severity to the stress and is usually consistent with our past reactions to similar events. Not surprisingly, different people will have different reactions to similar circumstances, but there is usually a commonality in reactions to life events across people. At its essence the life story perspective is about understanding our mental well-being as being connected with life events that have affected us in a way that is understandable to other humans.

When we seek professional help, we need to make sure that the clinician understands what we have encountered and how it has affected us. It is only human to come up with meaningful explanations—whether they are true or not—as a way of making sense of our experiences, especially in cases of random acts of violence or tragedy. So, it is also important to share with the clinician any stories we have told ourselves about why these events happened to us. The life story perspective operates on the basis of three elements that figure in many books, TV shows, and films: setting, sequence, and outcome: X happened to me then because of Y.

"I had a fender bender last night because I had too much to drink and wasn't as attentive as usual."

"My mother died prematurely because I didn't fight hard enough with her doctors to give her better care."

"I have cancer because God is punishing me."

A clinician treats the distress life events can cause by helping patients organize these events into a narrative that is more effective, active, and optimistic than the ones patients may have been telling themselves. The story you create together should make you feel better, not worse, about yourself and your situation. (The idea that you have to feel worse in the short-run in order to feel better in the long run is an unfortunate myth that has caused much prolongation of suffering.)

This healthier interpretation of the meaning of your life events—forged collaboratively between you and your clinician—should help you move forward in life. Notably, this perspective can help you cope with any physical illness (like cancer) or mental disease (like schizophrenia or bipolar disorder) by offering you alternative ways to think about your life, what we in the profession call "rescripting."

Self-Reflection

Write down the life stories you use to explain something that has happened to you. Follow the setting/sequence/outcome format and also reflect on what a Hollywood director making a film about your life might call an "alternate ending."

In this exercise, the **setting** is where we note the time and place and set the scene.

Sequence explains what happened and when.

The **outcome** addresses the questions what did this lead to and how did you feel as a result?

Finally, consider an alternative: other ways to interpret these events and describe what happened to you.

Here's an example of a life story told to me by one of my patients, one that I often hear.

Setting: "At the beginning of my junior year of college, I had already been living with my boyfriend for almost two years."

Sequence: "Right after the semester began, he started hanging out with this cute little blonde who lived in a dorm near ours. I saw them arm in arm one day on the quad, and I was trying to figure out how to deal with the situation, when he called me and broke up with me."

Outcome: "I was devastated. He was my first real boyfriend, and I couldn't imagine ever finding another guy I would feel the same way about. I blamed myself for the break-up. 'I deserved this,' I told myself. 'I didn't pay enough attention to him.' And I was sure the fact that I'd gained ten pounds since we first met was part of it. Plus, I didn't want to go out as much as we used to. That new girlfriend of his was always up for a party and she looked a lot better than me in a tight pair of jeans. Compared to her, I told myself, 'I'm fat and frumpy, and boring.'"

Alternative: "The truth is, we were still very young and moving in different directions. I was starting to get more serious about my studies and my life, and at that point he was still just looking for a little . . . well, for a little blonde who looked good in tight jeans. Could I have done things differently? Probably. But he was the one who broke off the relationship, and it had more to do with what he wanted, than with what I was or wasn't doing. Also, I look back at photos of myself from that period, and I realize that I really wasn't 'fat' or 'frumpy'!"

What's your story?

Setting:

Sequence:

Outcome:

Alternative:

The Dimensional Perspective

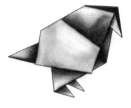 The dimensional perspective considers how our mental well-being or mental illness arises from aspects of our personality that make us resilient or vulnerable in specific situations.

We all think we know what the word "personality" means. We usually think of it as referring to someone who is bubbly or someone who is a killjoy. In psychological terms, our personality has two aspects: cognition and temperament, which essentially is the way you think and the way you feel.

Each of these aspects, in turn, has several dimensions, all of which are universal, measurable, and graded. Think of them as the psychological equivalents to physical characteristics such as height, weight, skin tone, and hair color.

For example, the cognitive dimension of intelligence is universal (each of us has more or less of it), measurable (it is usually gauged by IQ), and graded (it lies at some point on a spectrum), just like the dimension of height. We all have more or less height, and it's usually measured in feet and inches and exists on a spectrum (think of those growth charts in your doctor's office or that your parents drew on your bedroom wall when you were a child).

Also, like height, intelligence develops early in our life and stabilizes by early adulthood. As with our height, a slight decline in intelligence occurs when we become older adults, followed by accelerated decline in later life (even in the absence of dementia).

In addition to cognitive dimensions like intelligence, we also have temperament dimensions, five of them in fact, that follow the same normal distribution as height and intelligence. The "big five" are neuroticism, extraversion, openness, agreeableness, and conscientiousness.

Neuroticism is high in the case of a person who is very anxious, hostile, depressed, self-conscious, impulsive, and vulnerable.

An example of a highly neurotic person is the character Larry David in *Curb Your Enthusiasm*, who worries constantly and is always talking about himself and his problems. An example of a not very neurotic person is Leonard Nimoy's cool, detached Mr. Spock in the TV series *Star Trek* (Zachary Quinto's similarly dispassionate Mr. Spock in the newer series of "Star Trek" movies is an up-to-date version of the original).

Extraversion is high in a person who is warm, gregarious, assertive, and active and who seeks excitement and experiences positive emotions. If you are extraverted, you likely are an in-the-moment, life-of-the-party person, while if you are an introvert, you are probably more of a cautious wallflower.

Openness can either be very high in the case of a person with an overactive imagination, high aesthetic sensitivity, overattentiveness to inner feelings, high preference for variety, and high intellectual curiosity.

Or openness can be very low in the case of a person who does not think outside the box, who is not interested in taking risks, and who prefers to stick to a routine.

Agreeableness can also be very high, as in a person who is inclined to overly trust others, who is overly direct and straightforward, highly altruistic, overly compliant, extremely modest, and tender-minded or very low, as in a person who is suspicious, self-centered, distrustful, inflexible, and impatient.

Finally, **conscientiousness** is likewise understood as being either high or low—it is considered very high in the case of a person who is highly competent, extremely orderly, dutiful, over-achieving/striving, intensely self-disciplined, and very deliberate and perceived as very low in a person who is not self-motivated/driven and is not a planner and who is disorganized and doesn't follow through on promises.

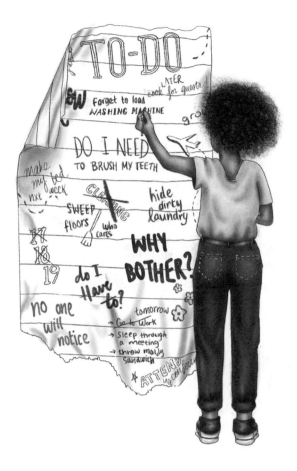

These aspects of your personality also stabilize by early adulthood. However, unlike height and intelligence, the temperament dimensions remain fairly stable even as we age. Thus, if you were generally a compliant, agreeable sixteen-year-old, chances are you're still likely to be that way when you're sixty-six.

But while you may not be able to change your temperament dimensions—it will be a natural impulse for you to feel a certain way—you can control the way you think and act in reaction to those feelings.

The first step is understanding what our cognitive and temperamental dimensions are. That way, we can better learn to leverage the positive aspects of our temperament to achieve optimal mental well-being and flourishing in our life.

At the same time, where we fall on the spectrum with respect to these dimensions can be a source of significant mental distress. For example, a person with slightly below-average intelligence growing up in a family of high-achieving parents and siblings might feel pressured by their family to do more than they are capable of, leading to feelings of distress, self-criticism, and bad behavior. Or a shy, introverted person might falter when put in the position of leading a team at work, interacting with employees, or giving presentations to upper management, which can also cause stress and anxiety.

Of course, one can also adjust to and overcome these situations: The person pressured to succeed could find their own path toward success, distinct from whatever professions their parents or siblings pursued. The shy introvert can put their feelings aside, rise to the occasion, and learn to be a better communicator.

If we fall on the extreme of a dimension, however, circumstances can lead us toward a pattern of what we psychiatrists call "maladaptive behavior."

For example, a person with extremely high intelligence may not be able to relate as well to those of us who may lack their intellectual gifts. That person could get frustrated over our inability to grasp the details of particle physics and thus become distressed about their ability to relate to others.

Those at the extremes of cognitive and temperamental dimensions often seek out treatment, and if the clinician is using *DSM* terminology, a diagnosis of "personality disorder" may be given. But this is where that "field guide" approach may fail. Dimensional characteristics can play a role in *many* psychiatric conditions, even in individuals who do not rest on the extremes and who do not have personality disorders by *DSM* criteria.

Understanding our dimensional characteristics can help us navigate life to achieve mental well-being and happiness, and—if one is in treatment—can help our clinician guide us in psychotherapy. The key concepts of the dimensional perspective are **potential** (to what degree we exhibit a particular attribute), provocation (the specific circumstance that we encounter), and response (the feelings, thoughts, and behaviors that result from the interaction between potential and provocation).

So, for example, John has a tendency to be impatient when driving. A high volume of traffic is a trigger for him, and he often responds by getting anxious ("I'm going to be late") and frustrated with himself ("Why didn't I plan this better? I should have left earlier or taken another route") and at times by expressing these emotions by cursing aloud, pounding on the steering wheel, and yelling out his car window at those not deemed to be driving fast enough.

In this perspective, our mental well-being and happiness depend on a good fit between who we are as a person—our personality—and our circumstances. Even if our cognitive and temperamental dimensions are part of our nature, we can notice, anticipate, manage, and possibly avoid circumstances that provoke our distress. And even if we can't change the circumstances, we can, as noted, change the way we think and act in response to those feelings.

So, to go back to our example of the impatient driver, instead of honking the horn, flipping off the driver, or thinking negative thoughts about the idiots on the road, John can instead say something like, "Okay, I'm angry, but this will pass, let's turn on some music and chill."

Successful flourishing requires you to be aware of your specific personality, accept this as the gift of individuality it is, and develop a plan to make the most of your personality by recognizing and avoiding certain provocations or learning how to better change our responses to them.

Self-Reflection

Document the potential strength of your feelings in general, a provocation likely to trigger a specific feeling, and the way you might typically think or act in response to that feeling or provocation.

For example, one of my patients, a female attorney, found herself struggling with what she identified as a "hot button" issue. Whenever one of the law firm partners criticized her, she became infuriated. In reflecting on this feeling and its triggers, she discovered that her potential was a tendency to be overly sensitive: "I take things hard. I'm not one to just let things roll easily off my back." What provoked her was people underestimating her: "When people dismiss my opinion or don't think I'm capable of doing something because I'm a woman or they don't think I'm smart enough, I get really angry." Her response was to go to great lengths to try to change their minds: "I think 'I'll show you' and then I go out of my way to prove them wrong."

Now reflect on the strength of your feelings in general, what triggers a specific feeling in you, and the typical way you might respond:

Potential:

Provocation:

Response:

The Behavior Perspective

The behavior perspective recognizes that what we do today affects how we will act tomorrow. We learn that choosing to act in certain ways bring rewards and others punishments (or, perhaps more accurately, negative consequences) and that choosing to *not* act in certain ways can likewise bring their own rewards and punishments.

These rewards and punishments can come from within us (the feeling of exhilaration after running, which we crave when we are prevented from running), from outside of us (compliments from others on losing weight or negative remarks about us not fitting into our clothes when we gain weight), or a combination of the two. These gradually shape our behaviors into habits, in which the drive to act in a certain way is so great that our choice seems effortless or else that we make it without even being aware that we have. When we explain our actions using the language of choice, rewards, punishments, cues, learning, and drives, then we are in the realm of the behavior perspective.

This perspective helps explain typical human behaviors, like eating, sleeping, and sex, as well as less common behaviors like substance use and gambling. Because eating, sleeping, and sex are all necessary to perpetuate the species, our bodies are physically structured in a way to support the cycles of these normal human desires. We become hungry for food, we eat a meal, our appetite is sated (a reward), and gradually we crave food again.

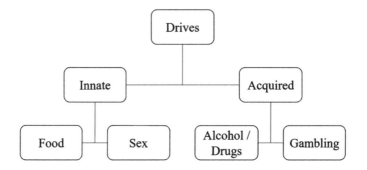

The human physiology that supports these everyday desires and the learning that comes with the associated rewards and punishments can be "hijacked." When this happens, we may develop unhealthy habits related to eating, sleeping, sex, substance use, or gambling, to the increasing exclusion of other, more normal behaviors. As the cycle continues, these bad habits may take over our life to the point that it separates us from our family and friends, and affects our job or school performance. At the same time, by virtue of habit, we have less ability to choose *not* to engage in the behavior. We become stuck in a cycle of repetitively engaging in the behavior in order to meet what is now a strongly desired goal.

For instance, if a person has anorexia nervosa, they choose not to eat to achieve the goal of what they perceive as being thin. In opioid use disorder, the choice is to ingest the drug, initially to achieve the goal of an altered mental state. This cycle becomes a habit in part by specific rewards (euphoria), avoidance of punishment (drug withdrawal), and cues associated with the behavior (seeing the drug). At the onset of any deleterious habit, our brains may be completely normal. A "broken part" of the brain is not necessary to explain the onset nor the continuation of the problem. The key concepts behind the behavior perspective are choice, physiological drive (desire), and conditioned learning (rewards, punishments, cues).

In essence, a behavior is something you do, an action. Treatment of behavioral disorders consists of applying the rules learned from the science of conditioned learning to stop that action. This begins with interrupting the problematic behavior for a sufficiently long time that the drive gradually diminishes and eventually recedes. If your daily routine of a morning latte at the local café—a behavior that is usually only problematic if you can't afford such a luxury—suddenly gets interrupted (whether due to lack of funds or a pandemic or both), you might really miss that steaming cup of java for a few days. But with time the urge for it will diminish. But for the urge to diminish it is also necessary to limit exposure to rewards, cues, or thoughts that may provoke craving for the behavior (like going to that café to pick up a muffin) and to put in place a plan to manage a relapse (typically inevitable in the earliest periods of interrupting any habitual behavior).

In this perspective, our mental well-being and happiness depend on the habits we develop. Learning to flourish consists of recognizing our ability to set goals that will support our mental well-being and happiness and to make choices that help us achieve those goals. If we find we are developing habits that are leading us away from our goals or if what we desire does not support our mental well-being and happiness, we will need to stop doing what we are doing long enough for the unhealthy desire to go away. We will also need to avoid certain rewards, cues, or thoughts that were part of the habit and put in place a plan to manage any relapse into our old patterns of behavior.

For example, if my goal is to lose weight, but I have a habit of eating a bowl of ice cream each night, what I need to do is figure out a way to stop eating the ice cream. But how? By keeping the ice cream out of my freezer, so I can't get my hands on it. To do that, I not only must not add Breyers Mint Chocolate Chip to my weekly shopping list, but I may have to avoid strolling the frozen food aisle altogether. And I certainly need to avoid treating myself to ice cream as a reward for getting through a rough day and to find an equally pleasurable reward for a job well done.

Self-Reflection

What action are you choosing to engage in habitually that is interfering with other goals you have? How strong is the drive pushing that choice? What reward do you get from choosing to yield to the drive? What could you be doing instead that may be more rewarding in the long term? An example of a choice might be spending hours before bed each night scrolling through social media on my smartphone where the drive to engage in this behavior is strong and the reward is mindless escape. Alternatives to this might be reading a book, socializing with family, going for a walk, or doing some stretching and meditating before turning in.

Now it's your turn!

Choice:

Drive:

Reward:

Alternatives:

The Disease Perspective

The three parts that make up the disease perspective include syndrome (the signs and symptoms that characterize a disease), pathophysiologic process (the process by which abnormalities give rise to the syndrome), and etiology (the pathology of an organ or organ systems that sets in motion the pathophysiologic process). Medical students learn how to talk to patients to gather the history and listen for symptoms of disease. They learn to use a stethoscope to listen to the lungs and the heart for signs of disease. Students quickly learn to recognize typical patterns of common diseases. For example, they know to suspect congestive heart failure (CHF) in a patient who presents with trouble breathing, weakness, ankle swelling, rapid heartbeat, and cough with pink phlegm. As they talk to a patient with these signs and symptoms, they know to ask about and look for risk factors for CHF, such as high blood pressure, coronary artery disease, or diabetes. Students learn which tests to order to confirm the presence of CHF (e.g., specific blood tests, chest X-ray, electrocardiogram, echocardiogram), and are often able—through these tests—to figure out why (the etiology) and how (the pathophysiologic process) the CHF happened. Based on an understanding of the why and how of a particular patient's CHF, students then know how best to treat and hopefully prevent future episodes in this patient.

Medical schools also train doctors like me, psychiatrists, to take a careful history, review symptoms, perform an examination, and recognize patterns of signs and symptoms for specific psychiatric diseases. As with nonpsychiatric diseases, students learn how to talk to patients to gather the history, listen for symptoms, and recognize typical patterns of common psychiatric diseases. But here's part of the difference between me and, say, an internist or cardiologist: I have no stethoscope enabling me to listen to the brain and no X-ray machine of the mind. The diagnosis of psychiatric disease relies on talking with the patient, family, and friends and using other sources of collateral information to construct the history and with the patient to "examine" his or her mind.

That's why it's crucial for you to track your emotional state, how you are coping with challenging situations, and any symptoms you may be experiencing and to communicate this information accurately to your clinician. You may want to use a journal or jot down notes to share at your appointment or check in. There are also apps like this one available to help you (http://www.wellocracy.com/mobile-mood-apps /mobile-mood-apps-chart/).

The essence of the disease perspective is that there is disruption of a bodily structure and/or function. In CHF, the disrupted function is the heart's weakened ability to pump blood. The most common cause of CHF is coronary artery disease, which results from the buildup of plaque in arteries, which reduces blood flow and can lead to heart attack.

In psychiatric disease, there is disruption of a brain structure and/or function that results in specific signs and symptoms. For example, we may see altered consciousness (as in delirium tremens), decline in overall cognition (as in dementia), pervasive change in mood (as in bipolar disorder), or an inability to integrate various mental functions (as in schizophrenia). Most psychiatric diseases have a typical pattern of signs and symptoms that—with training—is easily recognized. But given the complexity of the brain relative to other organs in the body, the pathologic process (how) and cause or etiology (why) of most psychiatric diseases are—compared to the rest of medicine—still a mystery. However, researchers are making progress.

For example, in the clinical syndrome of dementia—defined as a global decline in cognitive function that occurs in clear consciousness—we know there is structural and functional disruption of the brain. And in dementia associated with anemia and Huntington disease the respective causes are clear: vitamin B12 deficiency and a specific genetic mutation. Although how the genetic mutation causes the clinical syndrome in Huntington disease is not understood as completely as in nonpsychiatric diseases.

In the disease perspective, we see psychiatric illness that follows very typical patterns, with little regard to our personal history, personality, or behavior. Because the disease perspective assumes that a brain disruption underlies the patient's signs and symptoms, we cannot use it to explain psychiatric conditions more closely tied to our personal life such as the grief that accompanies the death of a loved one or the homesickness that can come with moving away from home.

This perspective cannot explain psychiatric conditions tied primarily to personality dimensions like neuroticism, and it cannot explain psychiatric conditions tied mainly to behaviors like anorexia nervosa.

Self-Reflection

There is little you can do on your own to modify underlying changes in the brain that may have led to your disease. But that doesn't mean you're helpless: daily exercise, avoiding substance use, getting a good night's sleep, and getting out of bed during the day are all behaviors that can help you, regardless of your illness.

And of course, you *can* and should get professional help. Indeed, asking for help starts with a recognition that help might be needed.

Are you experiencing (or are your loved ones suggesting that you are experiencing) an uncharacteristic, sustained, and pervasive change in your feelings, thoughts, and/or actions? If so, you may benefit from an evaluation by a health professional who can make sure that if you have a potentially treatable psychiatric disease, you get the treatment you need.

Now I hasten to add that not all changes are worrisome (changing your hairstyle or what you eat for breakfast, for example, are not normally alarm bells). But if the new behaviors are strikingly out of character or out of line with widely accepted norms, then they may be cause for concern.

Tying It All Together

No single perspective can fully explain anyone's psychiatric condition, which is why at Johns Hopkins, we use a holistic approach that employs four complementary ways of thinking about our patients. Taking a detailed history, conducting a thorough examination, and viewing the individual systematically from the four perspectives we have discussed in this chapter results in a more complete view of each patient. This in-depth understanding leads to a more comprehensive formulation and a more personalized set of treatment goals.

As I mentioned in the introduction of this book, a useful way to think of the four perspectives—although not necessarily in the order we presented them—is by the mnemonic HIDE:

Has (a person has a disease—the disease perspective)

Is (a person is a certain type of personality—the dimensional perspective)

Does (a person behaves in a certain type of way—the behavior perspective)

Encounters (a person is faced with certain circumstances in life—the life story perspective)

As we like to say, you can't run from mental illness, but you can HIDE! Now that you understand the four perspectives, you can begin your journey toward flourishing.

In the following chapters, you will discover some of the maladaptive (negative) stories you are telling yourself and begin to create for yourself a more empowering life narrative. You will learn about the strengths and vulnerabilities of your particular temperament and some alternative, healthier ways of responding to challenging situations. You will see how you have the power to change even the most serious of habits, including those involving eating and substance use. You will even learn to identify the signs and symptoms of the most common psychiatric diseases.

chapter 3

The First Step on Your Journey

Taking a Look at Your Life Story

The patient is a thirty-five-year-old female who presents with a chief complaint of "feeling really, really tired" for the past six months. She is married and has one child. She has trouble sleeping, despite her constant fatigue. She experiences periods of sadness, is feeling guilty about working outside the home, and is bothered by recurrent thoughts of the sudden death of her child. She has no known drug allergies or medical conditions. She does not smoke, drinks alcohol "socially," and denies illicit drug use. She tried to kill herself by taking pills once at age twenty-one. She saw a therapist two years ago. No other mental health treatment. One brother with bipolar disorder. No other psychiatric history in any immediate family members.

The female being described in these case notes is me, Meg Chisolm. And the life story I relate to you in this chapter and the next is truly mine, although I am mindful in telling it of protecting the privacy of some of my living family members.

I use my story to walk you through the process of evaluation that should happen at the beginning of any investigation into a mental illness. Perhaps you have already gone through this. Even if that is the case, you should know that, in my opinion, there is a right and wrong way to do it. This is not meant to criticize or second guess your current health professional. But having seen it from the point of view of a patient, a psychiatrist, and a researcher, I feel it is my obligation to tell you what I think are the best practices in this area. A proper evaluation, beginning with a thorough reconstruction of your life story, is the first step not only toward helping you with your current distress but in getting you on that road to flourishing.

If you are in distress, as I certainly was that day twenty-five years ago, it is always best to look first at our troubles from the perspective of our life story. Why start with this? Because it's the natural way that we humans explain our feelings, thoughts, and actions. We grow up listening to stories. We tell stories as toddlers, long before we learn to read or write. The stories we tell are not merely a chronological listing of events but real narratives in which we give meaning to those events that affect us most personally. Starting with our life story also prevents us from immediately assuming that every problem is caused by a brain disease, as is often assumed in our current era where neuroscience reigns supreme (in contrast to fifty years ago when the belief that every trouble was the result of an unconscious psychological conflict reigned supreme).

The elements of a life story—a sequence of events occurring in the setting of our life that affect our feelings, thoughts, and actions (i.e., psychological and behavioral outcomes)—are the same whether the story is about a fictional character, a historical figure, or about you or me.

This perspective is also a great place to start because it is in the context of our life story that our personality dimensions, behavioral disorders, and/or mental diseases occur. Although this does not mean your life story is necessarily the cause of these. Everyone has a life story that is unique, so in thinking about your own mental well-being and happiness (or that of a loved one), it makes sense to begin here.

I present my life story to you as a way to dig deeper into the life story perspective and to help you better grasp the process of how mental illnesses are diagnosed and treated (a process you may be going through now). Understanding this process can help you put your own experience with mental illness in perspective and enable you to see how it can be part of our journey to flourishing.

Given all that, the description of me at the beginning of this chapter might seem like a rather cursory version of my story. Unfortunately, clinicians often adopt a "Cliffs Notes" approach to a patient's life story and in so doing can end up misdiagnosing that patient and ultimately fail to help them.

To understand my situation, you would have needed to know a lot more about me than the fact that I was feeling extremely fatigued at night.

To understand the possible sources of my distress, you would have needed to spend considerable time talking with me. While that may sound obvious, this most basic interaction is sometimes rushed or overlooked by some professionals: to understand your distress, your health professional first needs to spend time speaking with and listening you. This is true whether that professional is a physician, psychologist, nurse practitioner, clinical social worker, physician's assistant, or other counselor. And the more you can tell them about yourself and your situation, the better (which is why you might want to keep and bring a journal of your thoughts, feelings, and actions or—better yet—bring in a loved one who can give their perspective on what is happening to you).

Let's break it down a bit further. There are four main things to expect from your mental health professional at this stage. They should

> take a detailed history (which is important to do, even in busy clinical settings such as a hospital emergency department),
>
> include information from multiple sources (not just you) in that history,
>
> perform a systematic mental status examination (MSE), and
> differentiate between observations and interpretations (which

means, for instance, avoiding inferring an emotional state from observations that don't support such an inference).

The multisourced MSE and its interpretation lay the groundwork for a clinician to look at you as a whole person, which is essential for them to determine whether your distress is arising from what you have encountered (the life story perspective), who you are (the dimensional perspective), what you are doing (the behavior perspective), and/or what you have (the disease perspective). Let's look at those elements a little more closely.

A Detailed History

A detailed history is not unique to the perspectives approach, although the first director of the Psychiatry Department at Johns Hopkins, the aforementioned Dr. Adolf Meyer, was the one who developed its format, which became standard practice. Now, however, many clinicians spend less time getting to know each patient—even in practice settings that are not particularly harried—and rely instead on the checklist approach to screen for psychiatric conditions defined in the *Diagnostic and Statistical Manual* (*DSM*). A detailed history takes more time, and it may no longer seem that necessary if a clinician thinks they can look at the patient and simply match the signs and symptoms to those listed in the *DSM*.

Consider the version of my MSE that appears at the opening of this chapter. It reduces complex problems of feelings, thoughts, and actions to overly simplistic disease categories, in this case the *DSM* diagnosis of "major depressive disorder."

Sad feelings, check.

Insomnia, check.

Fatigue, check.

Feelings of guilt, check.

Recurrent thoughts of death, check.

Bingo, diagnosis! She's got major depressive disorder.

No need to find out about parents, upbringing, experiences, about . . . well, a person's whole life. Who has time for that? Let's give them a prescription so they can sleep better. Next patient, please!

Okay, I'm exaggerating, but perhaps only slightly. This trend toward taking a less comprehensive history appeals to clinicians who—in addition to working in the age of the *DSM*—are also often working under the time constraints of managed health care and under the cultural influence of the pharmaceutical industry, who always have a pill at the ready for whatever ails you, mentally or physically.

You didn't know me twenty-five years ago, but I can assure you that my life and my feelings—good and bad—at that point, were, like most people's, quite complex. There was certainly a lot more that was going on with me than the simple fact that I was tired.

Allowing your story to unfold in a sequential way makes it more likely that your clinician will see you as that whole person (and appreciate how you as an individual have responded in different circumstances to life's challenges). This sequential unfolding can provide your clinician with a deeper understanding of the nature and origin of your distress. They are less likely to misunderstand your present condition as emerging simply from the pressure of your present circumstances. A more complete formulation of you and a more personalized treatment plan naturally arise from such a detailed history.

If you have already received a diagnosis without providing this information, bring it to your next visit. Clinicians make diagnoses of almost all mental conditions based on the history you provide and the MSE they perform, so the more information you can bring, the more accurate your diagnosis will be (and the more accurate your diagnosis is, the more successful your treatment will be).

Remember, there is no "gold standard" test to confirm a diagnosis, so this is a joint process informed by ongoing communication between you and your clinician.

Multiple Sources of Information

Your health professional needs to obtain information from a variety of sources in order to understand how others see you and your history. Speaking to family, friends, and even other clinicians who know you will allow them to form a more complete understanding of you and your condition.

I encourage you to find a clinician who includes a friend, family member, and/or another clinician in their evaluation of you, even if you are an adult seeking individual outpatient psychotherapy. In my experience, most patients and their family members are receptive to and appreciative of these discussions. Friends and family want to help. Early on in my career, I did not always make these contacts as part of the initial evaluation, but—over time—I have come to appreciate their value in understanding the nature and origin of my patients' troubles.

Mental Status Exam

The third essential feature of the psychiatric evaluation is the MSE, a systematic and structured assessment of what you are feeling, thinking, and doing. Think of it as the psychological equivalent of a physical examination your doctor would do if you went to see them with a problem. This enables a health professional to understand the nature and origin of your distress. Just as a doctor listens to a patient's heart and lungs in a certain order to learn what is normal and to avoid missing any abnormality, a good health professional will conduct the same MSE in a specific sequence.

This should not be an exercise in free association. Avoiding free association minimizes the chances that your clinician will miss any abnormality in your mental life. Nor should the MSE be an examination of your unconscious. No one—not you nor any psychiatrist—is a mind reader.

The MSE should be a structured yet empathic conversation that helps your clinician identify any unusual mental phenomena (e.g., hallucinations, delusions, obsessions) you may be experiencing while at the same time enables them to discover what it is like to walk in your shoes. Such an MSE can easily take twenty to thirty minutes, which is about the same amount of time as a thorough physical examination. Be patient with the process. It is worth investing the time up front so that your diagnosis is the most accurate it can be, because if it is, chances are your treatment will be more successful.

Observations before Interpretations

Explanations for past and current feelings, thoughts, actions, and events should not be disregarded; however, at times, your clinician may offer alternative explanations to yours for your consideration. For example, you may think that not doing well at work has caused your low mood, but your clinician—who has frequently seen how the disease of depression can affect energy, concentration, and job performance—may suggest a different explanation: that your mood disorder predated your work impairment and actually caused you to underperform at work.

The bottom line is that a clinician can only begin to understand the nature and origin of your current distress once they are relatively sure they have procured an accurate history and valid MSE, the two components of a psychiatric evaluation. This is fundamental to putting your current distress in the context of who you are as a person and what you have encountered in your life.

You may be surprised, as you read further in this book, by the level of detail that a proper history goes into. A good history gathers information not just about you but also, for example, your parents, and not just about whether they were "good" parents. A clinician who is conducting a thorough evaluation will ask about their occupation, education, health, income level, and personality as well as their relationship with you. They will want to get a sense of the extent to which your parents flourished too, as that may have influenced you.

My Case History

As I have suggested, a good history will cover a patient's complaint, family history, personal history, past medical history, premorbid personality, past psychiatric history, and history of present illness and gathers information not just from the patient but also friends and family. In what follows, I offer a much more complete version of my case history in which my husband figured as an informant.

My father was raised by a divorced mother in rural Ohio. His family was poor. After graduating from public high school, he served in the armed forces and graduated from a state university with a teaching degree. He attended college on the GI bill. After working as a high school science and later technical college instructor, he entered the aerospace industry. He attended night school at a private university to obtain his MBA and rose quickly into leadership positions, eventually becoming vice president of a major aerospace corporation. He was a shy, generous, and hard-working man and had no psychiatric conditions.

My mother was raised by her parents and maternal grandparents in poverty in eastern Kentucky. She married my father shortly after graduating from public high school. When she was twenty-five, my mother contracted equine encephalitis, and her case was so serious that it required emergency neurosurgery, but she made a full recovery. For most of her life, she exhibited signs and symptoms consistent with major depressive disorder, for which she did not seek treatment.

I am the eldest of three children. One brother, Michael, was born three years after me, and at the time of this mental health crisis, Michael had a history of attention deficit hyperactivity disorder, manic-depressive illness, and substance use disorders, and he had been hospitalized for extended periods in psychiatric wards. My other brother, Mark, is twelve years younger. At the time he was living in Texas with his wife and two children. He had no psychiatric conditions.

In the extended family, my paternal side has a strong history of substance use, anxiety, and possible manic-depressive illness. One of my two paternal cousins took their own life.

My mother's family history is unremarkable. I have no maternal cousins.

I was born in Ohio, the product of a full-term, uncomplicated pregnancy, by normal spontaneous vaginal delivery (requiring no interventions that are typically associated with a birth injury). I was a healthy infant and child with few, if any, medical problems. My father changed jobs frequently and by the time I was eight years old, my family had lived in four different states (Ohio, Michigan, New York, Florida) before settling in Maryland. Within Maryland, we lived in three different counties. My mother worked outside the home for the first three years of my life, during which time my paternal grandmother lived with us and cared for me while my mother worked. My mother stayed home full-time after my brother was born.

My home life as a child was relatively unremarkable except for the frequent relocations and the disruption caused by my elder brother's mental illnesses. As I grew older, my mother and I frequently clashed over her lack of support for my academic aspirations beyond high school.

I received a good education, despite attending a different public school every year until my last three years of high school. I excelled in both the humanities and sciences and was always at the top of my class.

I entered the University of Colorado Honors College, using money I had saved while working summer and part-time jobs through high school. During my freshman year, I thrived scholastically. However, I had to quit school for financial reasons. After that, I spent a year living with my parents in Maryland and worked full time to save money to attend an in-state university. I then entered University of Maryland, Baltimore County, to study film, supporting myself with part-time jobs and relying on government assistance for food. I excelled there, graduating magna cum laude, and was accepted into graduate school in cinema studies at New York University, but I decided to apply to medical school instead, after I had completed the required postbaccalaureate coursework. (That's a long story. If you're curious and have the time, see https://clos ler.org/passion-in-the-medical-profession/from-film-school-to-medical -school-how-john-berger-changed-my-life.) I applied early decision to medical school at the University of Maryland, which I entered at the age of twenty-six.

After graduating, I entered Johns Hopkins University for the required four years of residency training in psychiatry, where I was chief resident in my final year. I completed residency at the age of thirty-three, at which time I was one month pregnant with my first child. During the year I was pregnant and then a new mother, I completed a fellowship in forensic psychiatry, working at the state hospital for the criminally insane and the medical office of the local circuit court. After completing my specialty and subspecialty training, I began working for a local private psychiatric hospital full time; at the same time I was also caring for my five-month-old son.

I have never been arrested, nor do I have a history of physical or sexual abuse, and that was also the case at the time of my mental health crisis.

I have had several romantic relationships in my life. As a teenager, I had the same boyfriend for my last three years of high school. At age eighteen, I became engaged to a new boyfriend (and my first sexual partner) that I had met at college, but the relationship ended when I dropped out of school. Between nineteen and twenty, I lived with a third boyfriend, but the relationship ended when he started seeing another woman. At age twenty-one, I fell in love with and one year later married Richard, whom I had first met when I was nineteen years old. Richard was a self-employed cinematographer at the time I gave birth, and he was spending approximately a third of the year traveling.

I was raised a Protestant and attended church with my family weekly. I became an evangelical Christian during my sophomore year of high school. After going to college, I no longer identified myself as Christian and did not attend church, although I continued to believe in God. After the birth of my child, my interest in organized religion began to resurface.

I have no known drug allergies. I have no medical or surgical history.

I am described by my husband as a hard-working but rather intense person who often gets a "bee in her bonnet" and can be perfectionistic and demanding.

I had few long-term friends growing up, which I attribute to my frequent moves. But once we had settled in Columbia, Maryland, I developed a close network of friends at Oakland Mills High School.

I tried marijuana early in my high school years but have never used it regularly. I tried LSD three times in my life. I drink alcohol on occasion but never regularly and never in excess. I have never smoked tobacco.

I had one episode of major depression at the age of twenty, which lasted several months following the breakup with my third boyfriend. During this period, I had trouble falling and staying asleep, lost twenty-five pounds from lack of appetite, was sad and tearful, had problems concentrating, experienced feelings of low self-worth, and impulsively attempted suicide via an overdose of benzodiazepines. I was treated medically for the overdose in a local hospital emergency department but had no mental health evaluation, and they discharged me with no psychiatric follow-up. Three weeks later, I used LSD for the third (and final) time and, surprisingly, within twenty-four hours my depression began to lift.

From the period of my university years until the birth of my child, I had had no other episodes of depression.

Other than having short-lived bursts of mildly increased drive and impulsivity, at no point did I have clear episodes of mania, hallucinations, delusions, obsessions, compulsions, or phobias. I have never been hospitalized for psychiatric cause.

I had an uneventful pregnancy, labor, and delivery of my child. However, my mood was elated after delivery, and I was unable to sleep, even when the baby was in the care the nursing staff, and so I was prescribed a benzodiazepine, which was administered for over forty-eight hours after delivery. The baby was not temperamentally easy and cried incessantly, but I was in love with him and a joyful mother.

After being home with the baby a week, my husband had to travel for work and—without any additional support—I was left alone with the baby for over a week, due to a snowstorm that prevented my husband's scheduled return. I was on maternity leave from my fellowship training program for eight weeks. A wonderfully reliably nanny cared for the baby in our home when I resumed my training.

I was an anxious mother, which I attribute to the fact that this was my first child, and I felt slightly sad and guilty and extremely fatigued, which I think was the result of my having returned to work. A colleague had lost her five-year-old son to cancer the previous year, and I had been increasingly worried about losing my child to illness or injury.

I was in a support group for new mothers—many of whom worked outside the home—and I began to realize that none of them were as fatigued as I was. Recognizing this extreme fatigue as a possible symptom of depression, and with my husband's encouragement, I decided to seek treatment.

Everyone has a life story that is unique to them. Now you know a little bit more about mine.

In thinking about your own mental well-being and happiness, it makes sense to begin with your life story because doing so will help you to see how your feelings, thoughts, and actions originate in something you have encountered. When we look at ourselves from this perspective, we might then ask whether our negativity is rising in response to life events.

In my case, my life event was a happy one. I had wanted to have a child for many, many years and had, in fact, been initially sidetracked from this due to my husband's ambivalence about having a child early in our marriage and later to the demands of medical training and limited (or nonexistent) maternity leave policies. I had an idyllic pregnancy and easy, uneventful labor and delivery. Having my child was the peak experience of my life. Yet despite all of this joy and fulfillment, the birth of my son unexpectedly disrupted my life course, and I needed to seek psychiatric help to grapple with the unfamiliar feelings and thoughts I was experiencing.

And yes, it was all stressful, and I was very tired. But in reducing my situation to a few symptoms, the doctor I saw—although helpful—clearly missed the multifaceted origins of my symptoms, and did nothing to help me make meaning of the experience. The life story perspective, with its narrative logic of setting, sequence, and outcome, encourages us as patients, family members, and health professionals to take a "deep dive" and to use the story method to help give meaning to a particular event.

Psychologist Dan McAdams offers another way we can use stories—or what he calls our "own personal myth"—to make sense of our lives. In creating our own stories—like any author—we make certain narrative choices. We decide—in the story of our life—who are the good guys and who are the bad guys (or gals). We choose which events—major or minor—to highlight, and we decide what significance they have. How do these events shape us? Do they make us stronger or more afraid? In his research on what he calls "narrative identity," McAdams asks individuals to divide their lives into chapters and to recount key scenes, such as a high point, a low point, a turning point, or an early memory.

While those of us in the mental health profession may choose to rely on a psychological theory to construct this meaning, in telling different versions of our life stories, we may not rely on any theoretical model at all. The type of story told is much less important than other factors, such as—if you are in treatment—the relationship you have with your health professional.

Because you likely know yourself and your life better than anyone else does, it is relatively easy for you to understand the setting and sequence in which your feelings, thoughts, and actions have arisen and to understand your personality from which these are emanating. However, a clinician will need to spend time getting to know you before they can possibly achieve that level of understanding of you.

Self-Reflection

Take some time to write down your history. What story can you tell yourself about the origin of your mental illness?

Here, for example, is how I identify those points in the story of my own crisis, that I just related. The setting is "Once upon a time (when I was a new mother) . . ." The sequence is "After many years of marriage and enduring the rigors of medical training, I finally had the baby I'd always wanted, yet I felt anxious, sad, guilty, and extremely fatigued." And the outcome is the stories I told myself, such as "All new mothers feel this way," "I'm feeling this way because I'm working," and even "Maybe I'm not a good enough mother."

However, in this exercise also consider an alternate take for your life story. Yes, in this exercise you get to rewrite your life! In a manner of speaking. Instead of writing a story where things go from bad to worse, you want to create a story that will give a positive meaning to what you have encountered, one that will restore you to a state of hope, mental well-being, and happiness and that will allow you—ultimately—to flourish.

"Rescripting" your narrative in this way—turning it into a story of redemption, growth, communion, and/or agency—is the goal of treatment for any psychiatric condition that arises from something you have encountered. So, let's try rescripting yours. To show you how to do it, I will start with mine. Let's take "maybe I'm not a good enough mother" from my original life story outcome and rescript it to "raising a fussy baby is challenging, but I'm doing a good job. Things will get easier but, until then, I may need to ask my family and friends for more help, especially when my husband is away for work."

I've taken a story where things had gone from bad to worse and transformed it into a positive story of redemption and growth. Now, it's your turn (remember to use setting, sequence, and outcome to structure your story).

Repeat the exercise of writing down some of the stories you tell yourself to explain events in your life and then think of ways to rescript those stories in ways that make them more hopeful.

I encourage you to share the results of your self-reflection (both your original story and the rescripted version) with your clinician. Once they understand what you have encountered in your life and are able to see how that fits with who you are as a person, they can help you rescript your personal narratives even further. As you build your roadmap to flourishing, keep the principle of the life story perspective in mind. And remember, there's a happier ending waiting to be written.

chapter 4

The Importance of Personality Types

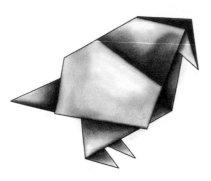

"Hi, my name is Meg, and I'm an extremely neurotic introvert."

Yes, that might sound like the way you'd introduce yourself in a support group (which many of my patients find highly beneficial). But there is nothing inherently wrong with being neurotic or with being introverted, the polar opposite of extraversion. Neuroticism and extraversion are dimensions of human personality, and recognizing where we fall on the spectrum from neurotic to extraverted can help us better understand ourselves as we move toward a flourishing life.

In the dimensional perspective, the underlying concept is that the psychological characteristics that together comprise your personality can represent a potential vulnerability, which under certain circumstances will be more likely to provoke unhelpful emotional, intellectual, and/or behavioral responses.

In this chapter, I continue to share more of my personal story to help you put your own unique experience with mental illness in perspective. Together, we'll consider how my personality (the dimensions of which I'll map out for you in a moment) when encountering specific life circumstances (the birth of my first child) provoked some of the symptoms of postpartum distress.

I'll explain how I addressed this and thereby provide a model for how you to address your responses to life's provocations by better understanding your potential vulnerabilities and personality.

The dimensional perspective encourages us to consider whether symptoms of mental distress, such as my postpartum symptoms, arise from a person's psychological dimensions, that is, out of who someone *is*. Like height and weight, these personality dimensions are universally present and measurable in each of us. Where you fall with respect to the various dimensions that make up human personality can be plotted along x- and y-axes, so you can see how you compare to other people.

This is one area in which we psychiatrists have objective and comparable criteria to work with. While we can't necessarily "measure" the level of your anxiety or anger, we *can* gauge aspects of your intelligence, for example, using the Wechsler Adult Intelligence Scale (WAIS) full-scale IQ score, which compares your intelligence to that of other people of the same age.

Thinking about your potential physical or psychological dimensions as aspects of personality that fall along a continuum can help you understand your potential strengths and vulnerabilities in particular circumstances. Again, compare it to how we view potential based on physical characteristics. For instance, if you are tall and slim, you may be well suited for basketball but not built to withstand the hard knocks of football. Similarly, if you are more introverted and cautious, you might make a good research scientist, but you'd be less likely to endure the hard knocks of steady rejections as a salesperson.

Just as your intelligence can be measured (and recorded as a point on the WAIS full-scale IQ), so can the dimensions of your temperament, such as introversion or extraversion. And for better or worse, just as with your IQ, your position on the introversion-extraversion continuum will remain relatively stable over time (presuming no intervening process like dementia or major depression).

A thorough history and MSE of the kind I described in previous chapters can yield enough information to allow a knowledgeable and experienced health professional to estimate your intelligence and temperament. This baseline temperament is also known as "premorbid personality," which alludes to the fact that "morbid" mental illnesses can have an impact on how an individual's personality might appear in an acute episode of illness. A person in the throes of nicotine withdrawal may become uncharacteristically short-tempered, for example. For this reason, no one should make assumptions about your personality or that of a loved one when you or they are in the midst of a disease process.

Although a formal measurement of temperament is not always feasible and/or necessary in the clinical setting, I have found the Neuroticism, Extraversion, Openness Personality Inventory (NEO-PI) to be clinically useful. The NEO-PI reliably and validly measures five aspects of temperament: neuroticism, extraversion, openness, agreeableness, and conscientiousness.

Here I focus on the introversion-extraversion and neuroticism-emotional stability dimensions because falling on the extreme end of these dimensions is the most common cause of severe mental distress. Being very extraverted or very introverted or being very neurotic or very emotionally stable can make a person respond to certain provocations in ways that are not helpful.

Introverts tend to take a while to warm up to others, to carefully consider the past or future implications of an event, and to have a slower emotional reaction to events. Extraverts tend to respond more impulsively, to focus more on the present than past or future, and to have quick emotional reactions to events that then fade just as quickly. Extraverts are more apt to be comfortable in social situations and to view themselves as "happy-go-lucky" and "spontaneous."

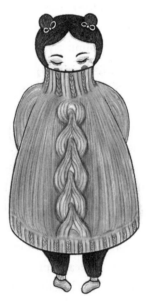

Introverts are not inherently "better" than extraverts (or vice versa). Depending on the circumstances, either can be an asset or a liability. For instance, if you are an introvert, you may not be the life of the

party because you're less spontaneous. However, your tendency
to think before you act may help
you avoid being impulsive.

If you are an extravert, besides
being fun at parties, you may be
well suited to certain careers, like
sales. Most extraverts, in the face
of forty-nine failed cold calls can
still make that fiftieth call. As an
extravert, however, a tendency
to live in the present can lead to
making impulsive decisions.

At the beginning of this
chapter, I referred to myself as
"neurotic." Although it's a term
overused in popular culture, this
dimension of temperament refers
specifically to the strength of a person's emotional responses to life
events. I happen to be *extremely* neurotic—meaning that, based on my
test scores, I literally fall on the extreme end of the spectrum relative to
the rest of the population.

Being on the extreme end of the neuroticism scale means that you have
the potential to respond to certain stresses or provocations with feelings, thoughts, or actions that may be disproportionate to them. A girlfriend of mine, for example, once sequestered herself in her room for
three days after accidentally spilling a drink on the lap of the cute guy
at work during an office party. This reaction to accidentally spilling a
drink is unhelpful to flourishing. Such responses upset a person's mental well-being and are often a good reason to seek professional help. Although I am neurotic, my testing reveals that I am only mildly introverted, which means that I might think a little longer about something I
said or am about to say but not to the point of ruination or social paral-
ysis like my girlfriend who spilled the drink.

Being aware of where you fall on the spectrum with respect to psychological dimensions—especially if you're on either extreme of any dimension—can help you understand the origin of troublesome feelings, thoughts, and actions when they arise and can also help guide your health professional's treatment of your distress.

Self-Reflection

Give some thought to the dimensions of your personality. Are you more past and future oriented or present oriented? If the former, you're more likely introverted; if you're very much living in the present, in the "now," you're probably extraverted. Are your emotions slow or quick to change? If slow, you're more likely introverted but if quick, then you are probably extraverted. Where do you think you lie on the neuroticism dimension? Do you feel your emotions intensely? If so, you're more likely to be neurotic.

Now take a free, abbreviated measure of your own dimensions at http://www.personalityassessor.com/ipip300. Do the results confirm your impressions or were you surprised by them?

People usually come to treatment when they are having difficulty navigating the ups and downs of everyday life, and this is often related to dimensional vulnerabilities. You may be experiencing trouble for the first time in the face of a new and unexpected life event. Nevertheless, regardless of where anyone falls on the spectrum of a psychological dimension, the potential to respond either positively or negatively to a particular provocation, including medical or psychiatric disease, is a fundamental aspect of human personhood.

In the dimensional perspective, it is the poor fit between who the person is and the circumstances in which that person finds themselves that drives the explanation of a given psychiatric condition. Where you fall on the spectrum of the two measurable dimensions of cognition and temperament can predict your potential to respond to various thoughts and actions, including life events, with feelings of sadness, aggression, discouragement, and anxiety. In my case, I have the potential to respond with strong feelings to stressors. And when I was faced with months of working outside the home each day and caring for a fussy baby each evening and into the night, which meant I was not getting enough sleep, I responded with strong negative emotions.

Treatment begins with helping you and or your family recognize who you are, relying on psychological testing, such as an IQ test or a personality inventory like the NEO-PI if needed to help you understand you better. Subsequently, you, your health professional, and your family can work together to set treatment goals based on this dimensional understanding of your presentation.

For example, guiding you to avoid situations that provoke distress may be a clinically relevant treatment goal. If, however, you can't avoid such situations, your health professional can help you manage the distress in various ways. They may work to strengthen your resilience to provocation by teaching you to anticipate provocations and practice responses. If you have a hair trigger temper that can lead to road rage, you'll need to figure out how to better manage and control your feelings of anger rather than avoid driving altogether.

If substance use is exacerbating your situation, your health professional may help you become and stay abstinent. Easier said than done, I realize, but trust me: it *can* be achieved. You can also be guided to avoid or delay (as you await a growth in maturity and judgment) exposure to certain provocations until you become more mature and develop better judgment and to modify your emotional responses via coaching or, in some cases, medication.

My Case History

I had been doing relatively well managing my life's demands. I had supported myself through college and withstood enduring the rigors of medical school. But in 1993, along came Clay. As happy as I was to have a healthy baby boy, I soon felt some of the symptoms of what I recognized to be postpartum distress.

This was not the first in my life I'd had trouble dealing with common life events. After the breakup with my boyfriend in college, I went through a difficult time. Think back to our "flow chart" of the dimensional perspective: based on my personality type, I had the potential to be provoked.

And I certainly was when it came to baby Clay.

I worried that a minor sunburn was going to scar my newborn's skin for life, that a routine heel stick to check for lead exposure was going to cause him unbearable pain, that not responding to every whimper and cry would mean I was a terrible mother.

I could fill this book with all the worries I had as a young mother.

You would think that a person who is today a psychiatrist would have immediately sought help. But that was not the case. I was hesitant to seek professional treatment, given the stigma surrounding mental illness and the further implications it had for me as a health care professional. Moreover, my personality came into play, which fortunately I recognized, having taken, as part of my psychiatry residency training, the NEO-PI.

Through that testing, I had learned that by nature I'm a highly conscientious person, sometimes bordering on perfectionistic. Accepting that I needed to seek help for that reason alone was challenging. However, in this case, my conscientiousness in combination with my neuroticism worked in my favor, as I wished to be the best mother I could be and it was that desire that spurred me to accept my husband's recommendation to seek help. Being slightly introverted, I am someone who thinks a lot about future consequences, and the last thing I wanted was for my untreated depression and anxiety to have lifelong consequences for my child, which it could have.

Another dimension of my personality helped me here as well. As someone relatively open to new experiences (remember that LSD experimenting in college?), I realized that this could be interesting as well as beneficial. I finally decided to take Richard's recommendation to see a psychiatrist for help. I was *so* glad I did.

I'll explain more about my treatment in the next chapter. But it's important here to see how understanding the dimensions of my personality —the measurable levels of cognition and temperament—helped me realize why I was in distress and that (with a little push from Richard) help was needed.

The results of my NEO-PI from nearly thirty years ago showed that I was neurotic, far more introverted than extraverted, open, a little more disagreeable than agreeable (surprise to me, but maybe not Richard), and very conscientious. The test's usefulness and reliability became really evident to me when I took an abbreviated version of the same test twenty years later. *Nothing* had changed—except of course my insights into my own personality. By that time I had learned that I could flourish, despite being mildly introverted and highly neurotic—which, I think it's safe to say, is how I will remain for the rest of my life. If you're interested in taking the full NEO-PI or a similar test, ask your health professional if they can provide that service or can refer you to someone who can.

chapter 5

The Role of Habits in Your Behavior

How did my own brother become addicted to alcohol and drugs?

As a psychiatrist, I now have a better understanding of the sinister combination of influences that pushed and pulled him down that path. But that question—*why?*—was asked by a lot of people in our lives at the time. If you're someone who is struggling with a substance use disorder, you may be wondering the same things.

How? Why? What could have caused me to fall into the grip of alcohol, cocaine, heroin, or opioids?

Michael certainly didn't grow up in a household where drinking was prevalent. My mother was a teetotaler; my father might have a drink but only very occasionally.

It didn't matter.

For my brother, the foundation of flourishing that the behavior perspective describes began to crumble at an early age.

In essence, a behavior is something that a person *does*. Behaviors are *goal-directed* physical actions. Neurologists and others study physical actions—such as walking, grasping, reaching, and running—and try to identify and explain disorders in these capacities to act. Individuals with

Parkinson's disease, for example, often have a tremor in their hands or can be unsteady on their feet as a result of degeneration in certain nerve cells in the brain.

Psychiatrists, by contrast, study how people employ those capacities—how they *choose* to behave—and seek to identify and explain disorders in these choices. Behavioral dysfunctions all involve goal-directed action but can be divided into three subgroups, or three different kinds of behaviors:

> disorders of innate drives (eating, sleep, and sexual disorders like pedophilia that are related to the most basic of human behaviors),
>
> disorders involving acquired drives (addiction, kleptomania, pathological gambling), and
>
> disorders provoked by a social attitude resting on assumptions, overvalued ideas, or search for a role (self-cutting, mass hysteria).

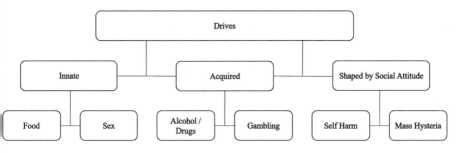

Behavior can be driven by innate, acquired, or socially shaped drives.

In the behavior perspective, the underlying conceptual triad is choice, physiological drive (development of a biologically based "hunger" for a behavior), and conditioned learning (which shapes behavior).

Drive is a brain-based physiological process that influences and dominates your other brain functions. It does this by producing an "attitude" that influences your perceptions and decisions. We all know the delicious aroma of a fresh-baked chocolate-chip cookie. But that doesn't mean you wolf down a dozen cookies every time you pick up that scent. You must make the decision to eat or not to eat one or more cookies. You decide whether to based in part on your attitude toward food at the time (whether you feel hungry or feel full). In this example, your appetite or hunger for the cookie is the drive.

Conditioned learning refers to how behaviors become habits, good or bad, based on associations. For instance, if you have insomnia at night sleeping in your bed, you develop a perception where you associate being in your bed with not sleeping, making it even harder for you to get to sleep (which is why it's often recommended that those having trouble with insomnia go to another room rather than lying awake in bed).

Drive and attitude alone do not determine your behavior, however. You know you do not always eat a cookie when you're hungry, nor are you always hungry when you do choose to eat a cookie. Choices to act or not are shaped by more personal aspects—what one has encountered, who one is dimensionally, and any brain disease one might have. Indeed, all the perspectives we've discussed in this book help determine our behavior.

The study of behavior, its nature, its role, and its dynamics, was a big part of twentieth-century psychology. Sigmund Freud appreciated the importance of drive in our mental life but was unable to identify a biological structure in the brain that embodied it. John B. Watson demonstrated that learning—via rewards and punishments—shapes behavior. Pavlov showed how, in what we now call classical conditioning, animals learn that one thing (a bell ring) leads to another (food), and B. F. Skinner, in his classic study on operant conditioning, demonstrated how animals learn that one thing (a lever press) *produces* another (food). Albert Bandura demonstrated that children learn what to do from watching adult role models in his experiment in which children observed an adult hitting an inflatable clown. When the children encountered Bobo the clown on their own, they—not surprisingly—also beat him up. At Johns Hopkins, Curt Richter identified a biological brain structure that embodies a drive shapeable by the environment. This brain structure—the suprachiasmatic nucleus—regulates your circadian rhythms, and hence your drive to sleep, which is influenced by the amount of light that reaches your brain via the optic nerve.

Taken as a whole, this body of research suggests that biological brain processes (derived from our genes) underlie certain behaviors and—most importantly—that the environment can shape these processes. It demonstrates what we all know intuitively: that nature and nurture matter. Brain structures function differently in different people, which is why we are rewarded by different things in the environment (some people try opioids and hate them, while others try them once and love them), why we learn differently (some people do better with the so-called carrot and others the stick), and why we differ in our ability to control impulses (think ADHD vs. OCD).

Individual differences in various areas of the brain help explain why people differ in how they behave. Problematic behaviors may result from physiologic "overdrive," such as that of a person going through a manic episode who displays an intense drive to engage in all kinds of behaviors, or from bad habits being rewarded ("maladaptive learning" as we call it in the profession) such as when parents giving in to their toddlers' tantrums teach their children to throw more tantrums, or a combination of the two.

If you've struggled with behavior change you may be skeptical that this perspective is something within your control or that you'll ever be able to flourish. Let me assure you that problematic behaviors *are* treatable, usually with a combination of medication and psychotherapy that helps us to "unlearn" them. While it's difficult to change a well-trained behavior, it can be done—sometimes relatively quickly, other times much more slowly. Regardless of where you are in your "unlearning" of a bad habit, you can start to flourish by making connections with your family, community, coworkers, and students and by seeking to put meaning and purpose back into your life. We'll talk more about how to do that in upcoming chapters.

Self-Reflection

What behavior whether innate (sleeping, eating, sexual, exercise) or acquired (gambling, drug and/or alcohol use) would you like to change? What rewards does that behavior bring and how might it help in your efforts to manage your mental distress? What—if anything—might compete with these rewards in both the short and long term?

Again, let me offer a personal example: my later-in-life battle against weight.

I was always thin, as a child and an adult. My metabolic "set point" made it easy for me not to gain weight. It was only after menopause that I began to put on pounds, suggesting that my set point had changed. That was the nature part.

The nurture part was the fact that preparing and eating elaborate meals with friends and family had become an extremely pleasurable hobby (if I may say so, my beef bourguignon was to die for). To put this hobby into the framework of the behavioral formula I've been discussing, cooking had become very rewarding, both mentally and physically, which increased my drive to make and eat these meals. I received compliments from friends and family on how good the meals were, which drove me to keep on cooking and to keep on eating the meals that had been rewarded.

You can guess where this is going. Yup, thanks to a little nature and a lot of nurture (and chicken cordon bleu), I gained sixty pounds.

I was now obese by any measure.

With the help of the Johns Hopkins Weight Management Center, I took action: I radically changed my diet and reduced my daily calories. In the short term, I needed to develop new activities that were equally rewarding, so I began walking daily and became passionately engaged in the preparation of healthier meals, made with local, organic ingredients. Over time I successfully changed my behavior. I lost a lot of weight: I went from a size 16 to a size 6 and dropped from 190 to 125–130 pounds (depending on if I have a glass of Prosecco with dinner or not), and I began feeling healthier and looking better. These benefits were their own rewards.

My own story of postpartum depression demonstrates only a few features of the behavior perspective. But my brother's story is, well, another story.

In retrospect, Michael had all the risk factors for developing a substance use disorder. First, there was a family history of alcoholism (in our paternal grandfather), suggesting a biologically driven "taste" for alcohol. Then there was Michael's diagnosis (in the 1960s, long before it became fashionable) of attention deficit hyperactivity disorder. All of this pointed to an inability to inhibit impulses (probably hereditary as well). And on top of that, he had a learning disability, making him a relative failure at school and that caused him to feel like he was a loser (there's the nurture part).

By the time he was in his early teens, he was already demoralized by his inability to succeed at school, despite being quite bright, and no longer in the protective environment of our parents' world, he turned to alcohol and later cocaine to numb the pain. Because of his hereditary vulnerability for developing a substance use disorder, once he started drinking, he developed a drive for alcohol that is just like the drive for food. He became literally starved for alcohol—a feeling many of my patients (and readers of this book) that are battling substances can relate to.

In Michael's story, we can see the operational underpinnings of the behavior perspective. He has a genetically derived vulnerability to the numbing effects of alcohol that went unexpressed early on in life, in the absence of exposure to alcohol in our largely teetotaling home. Once he made the choice to try alcohol, he experienced the immediate and striking effects of drinking and learned to associate drinking with these effects, thus acquiring a hunger for alcohol and a drive to have it. He then continued to drink to experience again these effects. Thus, his addiction to alcohol illustrates the underlying conceptual triad of the behavior perspective: physiological drive (the development of a "hunger" for alcohol as intense as if he was starving for sustenance or desperate for water), choice, and conditioned learning.

In other words, he continued to drink because of the perceived rewards of drinking and the "punishment" of not drinking.

My brother's genetic predisposition surely was not the reason he took his first drink, although genes likely influenced his continued use. These hereditary influences were powerful and overrode our parents' efforts and those of the criminal justice system (where Michael eventually found himself) to dissuade him from alcohol and, later, cocaine use. The persuasive influence of peers who encouraged him and provided him with opportunities to use were also part of it.

However, his behavior remained open to further influences. Shortly after his son was born, Michael went to prison on a cocaine charge (for the third time), which persuaded him to enter substance use treatment.

A good program will prevent illicit access to drugs and alcohol; you no longer have access, you don't use, and thus the reward gets extinguished as other rewards—making friends, renewed sense of purpose, feelings of hope—replace it. Also, medications can be offered to decrease drive, decrease choice to use, or block the rewards. However, it will take eighteen months at least to reset the brain so that it can experience the usual pleasures of life without the effects of the drug. In the meantime, you will need a lot of support, from family, coworkers, fellow students (if you are in school), as well as groups from AA to a faith community. These pathways to flourishing are also the pathways for recovery from behavioral disorders. It's a long march back, but it can be done.

Michael entered such a program. Once in treatment, he received further external persuasion not to use cocaine (and alcohol) and began to experience the rewards of abstinence. He reconnected with his young son, with our family. He made friends through his support groups. He got a job and began to find meaning and purpose in his work. In this way, he was able to learn how to manage his choices better. His genes may have influenced his behavior, but they did not *determine* his behavior. He retained the freedom to make choices as an individual despite the influence of his genetic makeup on his initial response to alcohol's numbing effects.

Although treating substance use disorders can be challenging, with behavioral and pharmacologic treatments, my brother was persuaded to give up his cocaine and alcohol use just as he was initially persuaded to try them. Part of the power that alcohol and drugs hold on individuals like my brother is that they satisfy in a way that mimics the satisfaction we get when our most basic needs are gratified. Many people who use heroin, for example, have compared the euphoria of their high to the experience of orgasmic release.

Because the experience of the positive effects of drugs is immediate, striking, and fairly reliable, individuals can become conditioned to want to repeat it again and again and again. This immediate positive experience can lead a person to continue to use even in the face of the negative experiences that accumulate with chronic drug use. Incarceration, loss of relationships, sickness—these are all negative consequences. The person with the addiction realizes this, but the glittering promise of the instant high achieved when using and the hardships posed by instant withdrawal when they stop makes it hard for them to act in their best interests.

The role of choice is what defines the behavior perspective, and it is usually the center of any debate about the role of the individual in behavioral disorders. Professionally, I have had a lot of experience in this area. I'm board certified in addiction medicine, and for ten years I was the director of psychiatry at the Johns Hopkins Center for Addiction and Pregnancy. Gaining an understanding of the concepts behind their addiction—the same principles I've explained to you here—helped many of my patients change their behavior—for good.

I wish I could include Michael's story among those happy endings. But that is not the case. Although he never went back to using cocaine, within three months of being released from prison—during which time, he had reconnected with a previous girlfriend who was also a heavy drinker—he started drinking again, which not only strained his relationship with his son's mother and his son but also threatened his job, which in turn, jeopardized his housing. In despair about his situation and feeling hopeless to change it, my brother took his own life—a radical cure for a treatable illness.

chapter 6

Mental Illness as a Disease

Remember our HIDE formula for the perspectives?

Has a disease
Is a certain personality
Does things and behaves
   a certain way
Encounters circumstances in life

In this mnemonic, the disease perspective comes first. But in our chapter-by-chapter dive into these four aspects of mental health, I have left the disease perspective for last.

There's a good reason for that.

Nearly one in five adults in the United States live with a mental illness of one form or another. If we examined these mental disorders through the perspective lens—the overall approach I take in this book—I'm betting we'd find that most are related to one of the first three dimensions and would include life story problems like bereavement, dimensional conditions like antisocial personality disorder, and behavior disorders like anorexia nervosa.

But the fourth perspective—disease—is different in several ways. First, please know that we use that term "disease" guardedly. In the age of the DSM (*Diagnostic and Statistical Manual*) with its array of categories and the numerous medications made available by large pharmaceutical corporations for the treatment of these psychiatric diseases, we too often rush to label ourselves or our loved ones with a diagnosis of bipolar disorder, schizophrenia, or obsessive-compulsive disorder.

Still, that doesn't mean there aren't lots of people out there with a diagnosed (and undiagnosed) psychiatric disease. Indeed, approximately 4.4 percent of adults in the United States will experience bipolar disorder at some time in their lives and close to 1 percent will develop schizophrenia.

A common misconception is that these individuals are so caught up in the throes of their disease and treatment that they are incapable of leading full and flourishing lives. And since you may very well be one of those individuals, it's important to understand this fourth perspective.

The three conceptual components associated with the disease perspective are clinical syndrome (that is, signs and symptoms), pathology (the malfunction or abnormality), and etiology (cause).

In essence, a disease is something a person *has* and that comes on them unbidden. When a brain structure or function is disrupted, symptoms of psychiatric diseases emerge. These can manifest themselves in various forms, including an altered level of consciousness (as in the delirium tremens seen in alcohol withdrawal), a decline in overall thinking and memory (dementia), a sustained and pervasive change in mood (bipolar disorder and major depression), and an inability to process information and motivate oneself (schizophrenia).

As a physician, I was trained to recognize the clustering of signs, symptoms, and course that define a clinical syndrome, whether a disease of the brain or of another organ in the body like the heart as in congestive heart failure (CHF). I also learned to identify the specific bodily pathology (abnormality) generating the clinical syndrome's features; the ultimate goal of this training was to be able to find the etiology (cause) of the pathology and so a cure (no definition needed for that).

As I continued in medical school, I began to realize—with the help of senior clinicians and a legacy of scientific evidence—that diagnosing a disease was not quite as cut and dried as writing check marks next to a list of symptoms. I became increasingly able to discern what had gone wrong, to be able to recognize what specific pathology was at work in a given patient from among an array of possible structural or functional pathologies that can be at play in an individual patient presenting with the syndrome of CHF. I learned that identifying the pathology of CHF for a particular patient is not only relevant to curing that patient but also may be helpful in identifying the ultimate cause.

If all that sounds like a lot of med-speak, consider this example. I learned that a patient who has CHF may also have an inflammation of the pericardium—the sac surrounding the heart—which can, in turn, be caused by a variety of factors. In patients whose immune system is compromised, this condition—called constrictive pericarditis—can be caused by a bacterial infection. Treating the patient for the infection with an antibiotic may slow the progression of the pericardial disease and extend life. So by thinking more about the root cause behind the symptoms, a health professional is more likely to arrive at effective treatment for the patient.

Later in my training, I moved from hearts to minds. I learned that the same elements associated with the disease perspective (clinical syndrome, pathology, and etiology) also apply to the clinical syndrome of depression. Only indirect evidence exists that depression—a disorder defined as a sustained and pervasive change in mood, vital sense (sleep, energy, concentration, etc.), and/or self-attitude (view toward self or future)—is related to any malfunction or abnormality of the brain. Thus, unlike the clear linkages we can make in the case of CHF (bacterial infection to constrictive pericarditis to CHF), in depression we cannot make the connection between cause, malfunction, and the signs and symptoms.

So, if I'm trying to figure out whether a patient's disease is depression and not simply a response to stress in the patient's life, I will consider some indirect evidence such as heritability (depression clearly runs in families), recognizable patterns of symptoms (such as pervasive and sustained changes in mood), and response to biologic treatments (like medication and electroconvulsive therapy).

Although the core features of depression are disturbances in mood, it is common to see changes in concentration and attention as well. It is also possible to have an episode of a mood disorder without a change in mood. You can have a change in only vital sense or a change in self-attitude and your mood can be fine, yet you can still be depressed. This, by the way, is a common presentation in older patients. Or the change in your mood can be irritability only, without sadness, which is more typical among young patients. It is usually the abnormalities in attitudes toward one's self—the feelings of guilt, the thoughts of death—that are most distressing to patients (as indeed, they were for me, when I was a patient).

The second step required to link the elements of the disease triad is to tie the pathology in some way to the clinical syndrome. This is a lot harder to do in psychiatry than it is in cardiology or most other branches of medicine. We simply do not understand the nature of normal mental functioning the way that we understand the nature of the functioning of a healthy heart. We have yet to understand how happiness works, much less to understand the nature of depression.

In other words, we don't have a William Harvey. Until Harvey came along in the seventeenth century, no one recognized that the heart is essentially a pump. Physicians at that time had treatments that they knew could relieve the symptoms of some forms of heart distress, but they didn't really know why these treatments worked, because they didn't yet understand the amazing mechanism that is the human heart. Harvey figured out that blood flowed continuously in one direction and that the heart was a muscle—a pump powered by muscular contraction. In some ways psychiatry today is like cardiology pre-Harvey. While there are certainly treatments and medications that can be effective, we don't really understand in great detail how the brain and consciousness works when things are going right—or wrong. And until the Harvey of psychiatry comes along, it's likely to remain that way.

The third step in the disease perspective is improving knowledge regarding the cause and pathogenesis of the pathology. A mouthful, I know. Simply stated, it means learning more about the cause of the mental illness and about how normal functioning might have gone awry.

Unfortunately, in depression, this is difficult to do at present. Even when there's a clear physiologic antecedent for the onset of the depression, like the birth of a child or a left-brain stroke, how these events are associated with the onset of a clinical syndrome of depression remains unclear.

When we look at mental illness from the disease perspective, we do a little medical detective work to identify the etiology and pathology of a clinical syndrome. What we call "disease reasoning"—which we use to link a clinical syndrome to the process that causes the problem—allows us to produce a testable model from which scientists can develop a clear line of research. It is the basis for much of the progress that has been made in medical research and holds great promise for the understanding and treatment of many, but not all, psychiatric conditions. Disease reasoning deemphasizes the personal aspects of your psychiatric condition and focuses on common features of the syndrome seen in other patients affected by it.

But we also realize that even this is not enough.

As I've explained, at Hopkins we also consider the whole patient and their relationship to the broader world. Who is their family? How much education have they attained? What is their occupation? Which community (religious, athletic, artistic, or otherwise) brings meaning to their life? These four domains of life can make the difference—after their psychiatric illness is treated—between languishing and flourishing.

Self-Reflection

The perception of mental illness as a stigma, as something to be ashamed of, is changing in our society, but very slowly.

Even patients take this view: that somehow *they* caused this, that *they* are to blame, that *they* are a failure because *they* have to take medication. Why do they feel that way? Because they are—and these very words still have more than a whiff of opprobrium—*mentally ill.*

That's rubbish.

This is a disease, a disease that for the most part people experience through no fault of their own. Do we blame people who lead a relatively healthy lifestyle and then get cancer? No, we feel sympathy. Same thing here: you've got a disease, and in the vast majority of cases, it can be cured or at least the symptoms can be alleviated.

As part of your healing process, I'd like you to ask yourself these questions. What signs, symptoms, and course of a disease have you or a loved one experienced? What was the most concerning aspect of this? What prompted you to seek help, if you have? What makes it better and what makes it worse?

Think about your answers. Write them down and consider sharing them with your therapist.

The more insight you can gain into your condition and yourself, the more we can escape the stigma. And we can't truly flourish until we've done that, until we recognize that what you have is an illness like any other. With a little help—from yourself and a professional—this too shall pass.

And once again, I'm speaking from personal experience as both a psychiatrist and a patient.

My Case History

I was feeling low. Two months after my son Clay had been born, I found myself irritable and cranky. I couldn't sleep and had little interest in sex. I felt drained physically and tired all the time. I was also overwhelmed by a sense of profound sadness, for no apparent reason.

Although I was still able to function on the job and as a mother, I felt guilty and plagued by self-doubts. I was not enjoying work as I had in the past, and I wasn't enjoying motherhood as much as I expected I would. I was becoming increasingly socially isolated and at times even had fleeting thoughts of suicide. That was frightening—along with my husband's concerns—and prompted me to seek help.

I didn't want Clay to grow up without his mother.

In retrospect, I don't think my case was a tough one to diagnose: if a woman is going to have depression in her life, there's a 50 percent chance it's going to occur in the postpartum period. My signs and course were typical, particularly because, in my case, the symptoms began gradually, several days after childbirth, with no other identifiable cause. That's a red flag for the syndrome known as postpartum depression.

Fortunately, depression is a highly treatable disease. My psychiatrist prescribed medication. It took a few weeks before it began to work, but when it did, the world suddenly seemed brighter and full of possibilities again. I could enjoy a summer day playing with Clay under the shade of an oak tree. As he grew, we shared in the thrill of simple pleasures, like taking a walk in the rain, wearing shiny galoshes, listening to the roaring of the rising stream near our house, and cruising around the inner harbor of Baltimore in water taxis, visiting the art museums and the aquarium along the way. Even the Baltimore Public Works Museum was exciting to us. In my new frame of mind, street lighting, road maintenance, and trash removal were marvels to behold and better understand.

When Clay got a little older, we enjoyed lively conversations while walking to school together in the morning, and back in the afternoon. Life was beautiful again. And, I'm happy to say, despite life's ordinary and extraordinary ups and downs, it has remained so.

You might not feel that way at this moment. You might be at the beginning stages of your healing journey. If so, take heart. People don't usually stay in the acute phase for long. As was certainly true in my case, proper diagnosis is critical for moving from that stage on to recovery.

If you're not already in treatment, I urge you to take those next steps. I believe that most people can and do turn their lives around. I've seen it with my patients, and I've experienced it personally.

The Four Pathways to Fulfillment

We've looked at our minds, our selves from four different perspectives. Now we come to the four pathways. Each of these requires us to put in an effort, usually extended over time, as well as to take personal responsibility for the outcome. Each encourages and accommodates individual capacities and preferences, but each also challenges our inclination to want to hide in our rooms, to languish and allow a psychiatric illness to hold our lives in check.

There is much to be gained by metaphorically kicking ourselves in the rear and moving forward on the pathways: improving these four aspects of life can lead to happiness and life satisfaction, physical and mental health, a sense of meaning and purpose, strength of character and virtuous behavior, and close social relationships. As a field, psychiatry has been concerned primarily with restoring the mental health of patients suffering from a range of psychiatric conditions. But as you've heard me say, at Hopkins we have always been interested in something more. We believe that the physical, psychological, rational, emotional, and moral aspects of a person cannot be properly understood in isolation from each other. The four common pathways of human flourishing—family, education, work, community—are fundamental components in life. Incorporating them, in some way or form, into your life is how you flourish.

Let's look at what the research, as well as practical experience, can tell us about the pathways.

Family

Even if we have never met our biological parents, the vast majority of us grow up in some type of family context, which we refer to as our "family of origin." In addition, the vast majority of us (in the United States, 80 percent of adults age twenty-five or older) get married, thus creating a family of our own choosing. So being part of a family is a very common, although not universal, experience.

Scientists have found that family life, including being married, is associated, sometimes over time (suggesting a possible cause and effect relationship), with various human flourishing outcomes. For instance, marriage is associated with greater happiness and life satisfaction, physical and mental health, a sense of meaning and purpose, and close social relationships.

Conversely, divorce is associated with less flourishing in those same domains. Marriage also affects children who, when raised within the context of a partnership, demonstrate greater flourishing in the domains of happiness and life satisfaction, mental and physical health, and close social relationships.

The route to flourishing on this pathway does not mean you have to have a "traditional" family. Families are changing in America. There are more single-parent families, more families with same-sex parents, and more families with adoptive parents. Because the research continues to evolve in this area, we can only say for sure that if your goal is to flourish, connecting with or creating some kind of family ties will be valuable.

People also find families in contexts outside of even a nontraditional unit. The idea that community organizations are like families in the connectedness, affection, and support they provide to their members is a common one. Whatever family you have or can create—through friends, neighbors, coworkers, members of a community group or church, in-laws or like-minded individuals across a spectrum of interests—will help you in your recovery from an acute episode of psychiatric illness. Remember, though, that unlike family, friends often move in and out of our lives. Restrengthening existing bonds or building new friendships will also propel you as you continue your journey toward well-being and flourishing.

Self-Reflection

Ask yourself the following questions and write down your responses. How do you define family? How—if at all—could your family help you to flourish? How might you foster flourishing in your family members? And could you please just call your uncle in Delaware, already?

Okay, I was kidding about that last one. But sometimes rekindling these important family relationships is just a matter of picking up a phone (or sending a text). Here's an example from my own family pathway. It's hard for me to keep in touch with my brother in Houston, as we're so busy. But we're both football fans, and so he and I are now in the process of organizing a family fantasy football league. My brother, me, all the kids, cousins, and in-laws: it may end up being a new way for us to interact and bond. I'm sure there are similar ways you could create new ties with familiar faces in your life.

Work

People who are employed or who return to the work force report higher levels of life satisfaction and have better physical and mental health, compared to those who are not working.

While the relationship between work and character and virtue is difficult to assess (as it is more difficult to obtain employment if one has a criminal record), work has been associated with increased likelihood of close social relationships, as those who are employed are more likely to marry whereas those who are unemployed are more likely to be divorced.

That family and community also figure in the effects of work on well-being that researchers have studied reminds us that we should not view these pathways as separate trails but more as components of a multi-use path. Like such a path, our pathway accommodates many approaches, many styles.

This is particularly so in the case of work. The recommendation here is not that you immediately go out and find a nine-to-five job. Your age, your health, and other aspects of your situation may preclude that. If so, you could perhaps consider a part-time job, which would likely provide some of the same benefits but without the same time commitment. Don't forget also that these days, particularly in the wake of the pandemic, more and more work is being done from home. Virtual interaction with coworkers, customers, or others—through video conferencing and other forms of digital communications—is likely to help build relationships (although how they compare with friendships forged from face-to-face interaction is an interesting question, and one that I'm sure many researchers are now looking at).

You don't even need to get paid to get value from work. Earlier, I told you the story of one of my former patients whose volunteer work with animals led to a career. But even without it leading to a career, the benefits of volunteer work, particularly with older patients, can be comparable to those a person would accrue from working (minus, of course, the paycheck). Indeed, it could be argued that some of the character-building benefits of volunteer work—giving to others, providing service, being part of an effort that seeks to improve society—exceed those of a paid position designed purely to make someone a profit.

And let's not forget the work of homemakers and caregivers. I've found that a lot of people with psychiatric issues find an important work role within their families in taking care of older parents or siblings. You don't need to be a nurse or trained caregiver. Mowing the lawn, doing chores, helping older parents or relatives do the food shopping are all helpful. There are a lot of ways to define work—and in these cases you're getting the added satisfaction of helping someone else close to you.

Self-Reflection

How—other than through paid employment—do you or could you serve your family or community through your labor? How might they depend on you? What satisfaction might you get from a "job well done" in this domain?

I really enjoyed participating in the "Loaves and Fishes" mission at my local Jesuit parish. For over twenty-five years, Sue—the leader of this group—has spent Saturday nights driving a van filled with food that she and a crew of volunteers hand out to the estimated three thousand homeless people living on the streets of Baltimore. The sandwiches, soup, and fruit she delivers are a godsend to these unfortunate individuals. Being part of her volunteer crew was such a rewarding experience. Treating everyone with respect and dignity is a value I hold deeply, and it is a privilege to be able to enact those values through service.

Education

Nearly everyone receives some kind of education, although the depth, breadth, and duration varies considerably across populations. The scientific literature suggests that higher levels of education are associated with higher levels of happiness and satisfaction, although we know people with PhDs who are miserable and folks who never attended college who are happy and flourishing, so there are certainly many, many exceptions to that.

There also is an association between higher levels of education and better health, but whether education is the direct link is unclear. This pathway has also been associated with character and virtue, as several long-term studies have found that those with higher levels of education are less likely to engage in criminal activity. Level of education may also be associated with the extent to which a person feels that their life has meaning and purpose.

A person with higher levels of education tends to have more, close social relationships as well, and there is evidence that while education may delay one's first marriage, it increases the overall likelihood of marriage and decreases the odds of divorce.

The education pathway highlights that a part of our well-being arises from our exposure to learning. Once you or a loved one has recovered from an acute episode of psychiatric illness, building or strengthening education at any level will help you or them on the journey toward well-being and flourishing. This could mean completing a GED, pursuing an undergraduate degree or certification in a technical skill, going to graduate school, or even just visiting the local library or museum.

Self-Reflection

What does education mean to you? What kind of education do you think would help you thrive, or flourish? Has your education supported your own flourishing? What can you do—today—to broaden your horizons and learn one new thing? It could be trying a new recipe, reading an online article about a new topic, or doing a crossword puzzle in which you learn a new word or fact or two.

I recently saw the documentary *True Justice* about Bryan Stevenson, the civil rights lawyer. I was impressed and wanted to learn more about the origin of his passion for righting the inequities of our criminal justice system, so I'm now reading his book *Just Mercy*. Reading it has given me a new perspective on many things and introduced me to an exemplary and fascinating individual who can inspire us all. Isn't that part of the power of a good book, on almost any subject? I'm sure there's a topic that interests you, that you've always wanted to explore. So read all about it . . . and learn.

Community

The types of community that seem to have the most impact on flourishing are religious ones. Consider these statistics about faith and its benefits.

Eighty-four percent of people worldwide report an affiliation with some type of religion. In the United States, that percentage is slightly lower; 79 percent of people identify with a particular faith group. However, 89 percent of Americans believe in God or a universal spirit and 75 percent consider religion a very important or fairly important part of life. In the United States, 43 percent report having attended a religious service in the last week, and scientific evidence suggests that participation in religious community is longitudinally associated with the various domains of flourishing (again, the paths run close to one another).

Studies have shown an association between religious service attendance and happiness and life satisfaction as well as better physical and mental health, including greater longevity. Most notably, religious community participation lowers the incidence of depression (by 30 percent) and is associated with an astounding five-fold decrease in the suicide rate.

Interestingly, the evidence suggests that it is religious service attendance in *community* with others, rather than solo spiritual or religious practices, that most strongly predicts better health outcomes. Scientific evidence also suggests a longitudinal association between an individual's attending religious services and how much meaning and purpose they felt their life had. In terms of character and virtue, evidence suggests religion promotes prosocial behavior, and there is an association between religious service attendance and generosity and civic engagement. Evidence also suggests that praying increases an individual's capacity for forgiveness and makes them more trusting and grateful. Finally, scientific evidence suggests that religious service attendance is longitudinally associated with a greater number of close relationships, as measured by less likelihood of divorce, greater likelihood of making new friends and of marrying, and greater social support.

Given these findings, and regardless of one's views on organized religion, you have to admit that when it comes to helping individuals lead a happier, healthier life, it's a powerful force. It provides answers to life's "big questions," yes, but it also provides something more: a sense of community.

As with family and work, however, we need to broaden the definition. I think it's most interesting that the benefits of religious affiliation are found in group worship as opposed to those who seek a solitary path of spiritual enlightenment. This suggests that it matters less what we're congregating *for* than that we simply congregate. Again, as with family, if religion is not be your thing, you can create such an assembly not around God but other aspects of life.

Many of my patients are not religious in the traditional sense. But those who have gone on to flourish did find a sense of community in other ways. I myself am a churchgoer, so I don't mean to be impertinent or dismissive of organized religion when I say that belonging to a stamp collecting club or a Civil War roundtable or a video gaming group or that even the kind of cohesive community found among fans of college football teams or bands like Phish, can provide similar benefits in terms of flourishing as being a regular attendee at a church, synagogue, or mosque. However, friendships and connections developed in these other kinds of community groups who share a sense of meaning and purpose can be just as valuable, even if the greater feeling of purpose or meaning in life that studies have found reported among people who attend religious services might be specifically connected to the religious aspect rather than tied specifically to the community aspect.

Once you or a loved one has recovered from an acute episode of psychiatric illness, engaging or reengaging with a faith community—even if it's a faith based around shared passions or interests such as sports or music—will help you or them on the journey toward well-being and flourishing.

Self-Reflection

Have you been a part of a meaningful community in the past? What benefits came from that affiliation? What community might you connect (or reconnect) with now?

In addition to attending mass each week, I also like to hike and experience nature, and I heard there's a local group that meets at various parks in our area for moderately paced walks every weekend. I'm going to sign up for one. (Yes, the journey on our own pathways is an ongoing one.)

4 + 4: A Formula for Flourishing

Just as no single perspective can fully explain anyone's psychiatric condition, no single pathway can lead to human flourishing. This is why I use a holistic approach that employs four complementary ways of thinking about a patient's psychiatric illness and four complementary pathways that help them to reach their greatest potential and enable them to flourish in life once they have recovered from an acute episode of illness.

Viewing the individual systematically from all four perspectives and all four pathways results in a more complete view of each patient as a human being. This in-depth understanding leads to a more comprehensive and personalized set of treatment goals that aim for more than the elimination of illness. Mental health is not simply the absence of mental illness, but the achievement of well-being, or human flourishing.

In the following chapter, I share the details of the pathways I've taken and you will develop a deeper appreciation of where you are on your own journey to well-being and flourishing. First, however, here are two illuminating case studies of patients of mine who, after battling serious psychiatric illness, struck out on their own pathways—and, in my estimation—have come a long way.

Case Studies

Zack came to me at age twenty-two with a serious problem: obsessive-compulsive disorder (OCD), which in his case, manifested itself in the fear that powerful body odor made his very presence offensive. Zack was an athlete who enjoyed having  beers with his buddies and who was interested in meeting girls. But all that ceased because of his psychiatric illness. He avoided his friends, stopped going to class, was afraid of getting a job where he imagined that he would repulse coworkers. His life had essentially come to a standstill over what was a largely imagined condition. His mother told me that he had seen a medical doctor, who had confirmed that while Zack sweated like any normal young man, his showering and use of deodorant addressed that problem, as it does for most people. But in Zack's mind, he was an olfactory pariah.

Zack's illness meant that he could not accept that his problem wasn't in his armpits but in his head. He had to compulsively wash and shower all the time. He was racked with fear and worry and had essentially cut himself off from everything in his life.

I adopted the same program I present in this book for Zack. I used the perspectives approach to get a better sense of who he was. He came to trust in me, and over the course of a year of therapy, he made progress. Although skeptical, he entertained my suggestion that his thoughts might be symptoms of a disease and—because he knew his life wasn't where he wanted it to be—he agreed to try a medication for OCD. To his surprise, after just a few weeks of taking the medication, his worries began to subside. Eventually, he came to see them (as I had hoped he would), as symptoms of a disease and became dedicated to staying on this medication.

It was time for the next step. Zack wanted to get beyond the illness that had derailed his emergence into adult life. Now he wanted to move ahead. Now he wanted to flourish.

Zack was ready to strike out aggressively on the four pathways. The route he took highlights the fact that these pathways are highly individualized and often interconnect. He thought, and I agreed, that the first piece of unfinished business was his education. Because of his disease, he had never finished high school. "I need to take care of that," he said to me. He went back to a night program at his local high school and earned a GED.

The GED enabled him to get a job at one branch of a local chain coffee shop. One of his coworkers there was a lovely young lady. They started to date. At around the same time, Zack began to reconnect with some of the things he had enjoyed before he got ill. He remembered fondly how he used to fish with his dad (who by this point had died). He bought rod and reel and began dipping his pole in streams throughout Maryland. In rural Harford County one Sunday, he met some fellow anglers, and they invited him to join a local fishing club they belonged to. This tight-knit group of mostly men fished together on weekends, and periodically went on fishing trips to Canada or on the West Coast. I know some people will tell you that fishing, especially bass fishing, is like a religion to them. Well, I'm here to say they might be right. The River Ratz Bassmasters is not a church, but for Zack this group became his community and perhaps part of his extended family as well.

These days, I see Zack once or twice a year, and it seems that every time I do, nicer and nicer things are happening in his life. He was promoted to manager of one of the shops; his girlfriend, now his wife, manages another location in the same local chain. They recently bought their first house together. Zack has served as president of the Bassmasters, and, as he's now in management, he's thinking of taking some business classes at night at a local community college.

No two ways about it: Zack is flourishing.

This didn't happen overnight. It's been at least eight years since I first met Zack. The journeys through the perspectives and down the pathways often take time. And while he has blossomed, it doesn't mean that he doesn't also have setbacks. A year ago, his old problem began to resurface. Despite protestations to the contrary by his wife, Zack believed that his body odor had returned. We adjusted his medication and once again, it's under control. A reminder that all pathways zig and zag, but Zack continues down his and is a much happier young man.

Becca is another instructive example of how to navigate the pathways. She was in her early twenties when I first met her. Becca—like her mother and sisters—was always a little heavier than her peers. At college, she gained the usual freshman fifteen (pounds, that is) and started drinking alcohol on the weekends with her new sisters in her sorority. Those weekends soon began on Thursdays. Her binge drinking resulted in vomiting, which also for her meant that she threw up the dining hall food that was contributing to her weight gain. Liking both the intoxicating effects of alcohol and the slimming effects of vomiting, by the spring semester, Becca's bulimia—with its cycle of binge eating and vomiting—had taken on a life of its own, separate from her problematic alcohol use, and became serious enough that she required hospitalization and a leave of absence from college.

Treatment and medication really helped Becca. Three years out, she still doesn't feel 100 percent, but she's learned ways to cope with the fact that—based on her genes—she's never going to be as thin as society expects most women to be. With the help of AA, she's also learned ways —other than alcohol and food—to cope with the social and academic stresses of college life.

Once she was out of the acute phase of her illness, Becca went back to college and completed her degree. She decided not to rejoin a sorority; instead, while she was taking classes, she worked part time as a receptionist in a law office.

Like Zack, she met a partner there: a paralegal a few years older than she.

Becca, who was raised in the Jewish faith, also returned to synagogue as part of her alcohol recovery journey. In addition to this more traditional religious community, Becca found a new one: the local SPCA rescue shelter, where she volunteers. That group has also become like a second family (again, reminding us of the frequent overlap between family and community when it comes to healing and flourishing). Becca not only has a solid relationship with her patients but also with the friends she has made at the SPCA, who have made a big difference in her life. They even have a Thanksgiving dinner together—the staff and volunteers prepare a special holiday meal for the dogs and cats and then head out for a human Thanksgiving feast at a local restaurant. When Becca told me about how much it meant to her to be with those who share her passion for animals, I could see that she had found a new family on her pathway.

Zack and Becca's stories are illustrative, in several ways. They remind us that in order to flourish we need to take action. My patients who end up flourishing have made a decision—and not necessarily an easy one—to put themselves out there. They go to work, they join a community group, they do volunteer work, they try to stay connected with family or friends, or they develop connections with new friends.

During the acute phase of their recovery, people understandably become withdrawn or alienated. Just like most of us don't want visitors when we have the flu or a stomach virus, most of us don't want to be socializing or interacting with others while we're battling a psychiatric disease. But while that might be an understandable strategy during recovery, cloistering yourself in your room is not going to help you flourish. My patients who successfully navigate those pathways make a conscious effort to get out.

And traveling the length of these paths takes time. As I mentioned,

Zack's journey has taken eight years. For some of my older patients, it might be much longer. It's like what they say about becoming physically fit. You can't expect to get in shape in three weeks after you've been out of shape for three decades. Small, incremental steps are required. If you're reading this book, flourishing is your ultimate goal. But striking out on the four pathways is how you begin the journey. I'm excited to see what you will find along the way.

chapter 8

Your Road Map to Go from Surviving to Thriving

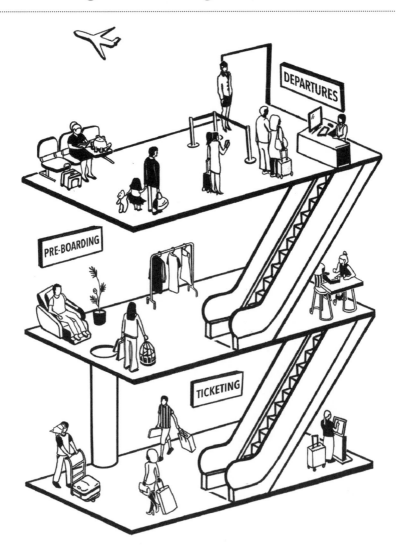

Think of the perspectives and the pathways as separate levels of an airport connected by escalators of thought. Your thoughts. How to gather them and then use them to take the kind of actions needed to flourish are the focus of this chapter.

At the risk of belaboring our aviation analogy, imagine the perspectives —the subject of chapters 3–6—as the ticketing level of the airport. This is where you go at the start of your flourishing journey.

Here you examine yourself from these four vantage points—the life story, dimensional, behavior, and disease perspectives. Remember the helpful HIDE formula:

Has (a disease),

Is (a certain type of personality),

Does (behaves in a particular way),

Encounters (is presented with certain circumstances in life).

These can help illuminate where you are at this point in your life, despite your mental illness.

In this stage, the focus is on self-examination: You're thinking about your life story and your personality. You're looking at yourself—where you've come from and where you're going. And if you have a behavioral disorder or a disease, you may have even taken some first steps (swearing off marijuana or committing to taking your antidepressant medication) toward regaining control over your life.

The top level, the pathways—the departures area, if you're traveling —is the more long-term, "take action" phase. Here, as we discussed in chapter 7, we seek to build new friendships, engage in meaningful work or volunteer experiences, and find a community with like-minded people.

It's from this level that you will soar.

For some, there is also an important intermediary step, which I'll get to in a moment.

But simply understanding the distinction between the perspectives part, which is more of a reflective and in some cases early action stage, and the pathways part, which involves the long-term commitment to more "doing," will help you harmonize what you do in one pathway with what you are doing in another.

The perspectives help you understand the origins of your psychiatric illness, and the pathways will help you make the most of your life (whether you have a psychiatric illness or not).

Let's go back down to the first level: how do you glean these insights and take the first steps toward getting your life back under control?

You can start, if you haven't already, by going back through the self-reflections we suggested in each of the four perspectives chapters. Don't rush through them. Think before you write down your answers. Even if you're currently in therapy, these aspects of your life are worth exploring. Your health professional—whether they refer to them as perspectives or not—will likely guide you through this process, which will help you to better understand yourself and better prepare you to take the next step.

While the thoughts may be complex, getting into a reflective, self-examining state of mind need not be difficult. Research shows that, in addition to many other benefits, physical activity can help stimulate the kind of thinking we need to be doing. I can tell you from personal experience that nothing is better for clearing away the mental cobwebs, putting aside the hurly-burly of everyday life, and starting to look at yourself in relation to these larger issues, these patterns, in your life than a long walk outdoors.

Preboarding

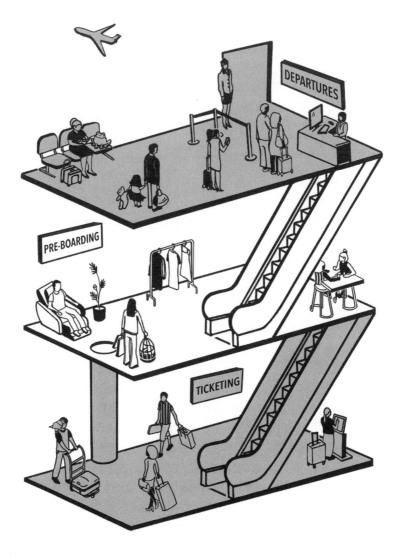

The perspectives give you a model for better understanding yourself. But now as we head up the escalator to the next level, we come to the intermediary phase I alluded to earlier. Think of it as the mezzanine level between ticketing and departures (perspectives and pathways).

You might need to spend time here working to resolve any impediments that could prevent you from making your way down the pathways. Meaning that if you're still in an acute phase of your disease, you cannot yet proceed to departures. If you have, say, an alcohol use disorder, you have to do something about that beyond thinking about or looking at yourself before you can start considering what actions to take on the pathways.

It makes sense: you're not going to be able to get a job if you're still drinking, and you may not be able to reengage with family. So those are two pathways (work and family) that are effectively blocked to you until you address the main issue at hand: putting some time between you and your drinking. Or, if you were dealing with anorexia, you should be at a point where you're steadily gaining weight, not just taking the first nibbles of food.

For some, the stop on the mezzanine may be brief, while for others it may be longer. Once you've had some success taking the necessary actions related to your particular illness, *then* you're ready to embark on the pathways.

Ready for Takeoff

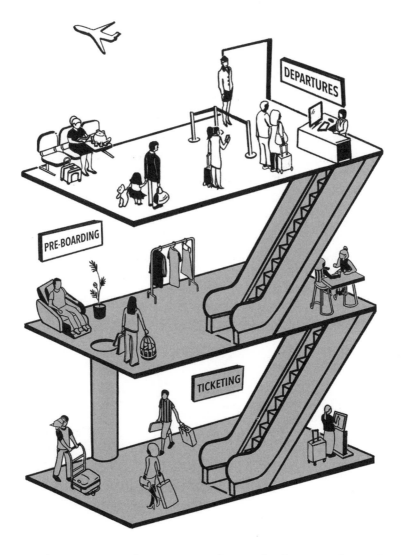

When you are ready to move to that top level, you might need to figure out which area—family, work, education, community—you are going to focus on first. Don't try to jump on all four paths simultaneously. You'll have to prioritize. If you need to pay rent, then quite clearly you need to get moving on the work pathway. Or, again using the example of the person battling addiction, you might need to fully engage in a new community through a support group like AA before you try to take steps on the other pathways.

In that case, the thought process might go something like this: "First, I need to stay sober, so connecting more deeply with the local AA community is my first priority. Only when I've stayed sober for ninety days or so, can I begin to reconnect with my family. And I need to remain sober in order to start applying for jobs. Maybe the job I get will come with education benefits that will allow me to start taking courses at the local community college, so I can finish my associate's degree."

Others in a similar situation may need the support of their family first. Only then might they feel comfortable joining a community like AA to ensure their long-term recovery.

There's no one-size-fits-all itinerary. Your goals have to be personalized, prioritized, and sequential. And one pathway, as we've seen, can link to another—often in surprisingly positive ways.

Here's how two of my patients, Sandi and Adam, made their transition from the perspectives level to the pathways—and then took off!

Case Studies

Sandi, who was around fifty when I first met her, came to me with a case of severe depression. In the perspectives phase, we spent considerable time on her life story, during which I learned that Sandi's father had died when she was only thirteen years old. Sandi had been raised by a single mother who was unprepared for and overwhelmed by the responsibilities of holding down a nine to five job while raising a child. Sandi was largely left to fend for herself during her adolescence. She did well, excelling in high school and earning a college scholarship. After seeing her mother's financial and emotional struggles, Sandi was determined to pursue a career in which she would be well remunerated. After her sophomore year, she switched her major from art and design to prelaw. After she earned her JD degree and passed the bar a few years later, she was hired by a prestigious law firm.

There, Sandi met another young associate. They got married, and the couple had two children. But soon fissures appeared in what, to most outsiders, probably seemed like the perfect life. Working long hours at the firm while trying to be a mom was stressful and exhausting. She began to question her life's path. Negotiating corporate contracts was a lucrative and highly skilled job, but Sandi had never really thrived in the practice of law.

Meanwhile, her husband had been lured away to another firm, where he'd become a partner. He worked long hours and traveled constantly. Soon, Sandi began to feel like she was a better-educated version of her mother—a single mom, overwhelmed by her responsibilities.

Depression often develops for women during menopause, and for Sandi, compounded by her existential crisis, it became severe. She began drinking more. She gained weight. She became more isolated, losing touch with old, reliable friends. She also started to resent the kind of lifestyle she had once aspired to. All the material trappings—she lived in a beautiful house, drove a Porsche, had a summer home on Cape Cod—now seemed as superficial as her affluent neighbors, who she began to despise for being entitled, rich, and shallow.

"I didn't grow up that way," she said in one of our sessions. "I didn't want to be struggling to pay the rent, like my mother did, but I know there's a lot more to life than sports cars and a stupid country club membership."

"Sandi," I told her, "you've achieved a lot in your life, and you've come a long way. You should be proud of that. But you need to figure out if that's what you really want."

Sandi, to use our airport analogy, was now on the mezzanine, but it didn't look like she was going to be there long. Looking at and reflecting on her life story had helped her make sense of why she was feeling the way she was. She also realized that she had been depressed, but that now thanks to medication and therapy, she was ready to move beyond her disease.

Before she could start on the pathways, however, Sandi needed to prioritize her goals.

Where was it that she really wanted to go?

This is what we worked on over the ensuing weeks. Eventually she was able to envision the kind of situation that would truly make her happy. She wanted her relationship with her husband to be more meaningful and intimate—not two successful individuals, seeing each other in passing, briefcases in hand. And she wanted to reconnect with her long-suppressed creativity. She needed to become the artist she had never allowed herself to be.

Now that she had her long-term goals, she was ready to continue up to the next level and begin to take her first steps on the pathways. She decided that she and her husband should have a "date night" every week or two (the family pathway). He agreed, and over an evening of spicy rainbow rolls and sake at their local sushi restaurant, they decided that a weekly dinner wasn't enough. They agreed to take ballroom dancing classes together, something they'd contemplated when they were first dating, years before.

Meanwhile, Sandi decided to convert an unused guest bedroom into a studio. To rekindle some of her artistic skills, she took a jewelry-making class, and a few months later, she launched a website on which she sold her beautiful earrings and necklaces. Sandi gave me a broach as a holiday gift. I treasure it, as a symbol to me of someone who, in midlife, finally found the pathways to flourishing she had always been looking for.

Sandi seems to have glided up the escalator from the perspectives to the pathways, with just a short stop in that mezzanine lounge.

Adam, one of my other patients, had a longer stay.

During the perspectives phase, Adam, by then in his mid-twenties, learned that in order to get over his opioid addiction he was going to need to get on medication. Once his mind was clearer, he rediscovered in therapy his extraverted personality. Despite the addiction that had isolated him from so many of his friends and family members, he realized that he had always been comfortable around people and that he seemed particularly adept at making them laugh. During one of his sessions, he recalled (for the first time in years, he said) how he had entertained his ninth-grade English class with his one-man-show version of *To Kill A Mockingbird*, during which he read the voices of both Scout and Atticus Finch and got a standing ovation.

Within a year, Adam realized through therapy and his self-reflections that his gregarious nature could help him on the pathways to flourishing. First, his ease with strangers made it easier for him to feel comfortable joining the community of Narcotics Anonymous. It wasn't hard for him to find a sponsor that he enjoyed working with (and vice versa), and he always felt energized after attending his daily meeting, which he continued to attend daily for nearly five years (he still attends at least once a week).

Back in touch with his inner thespian, he was now ready to embark on the work pathway. He applied for a job as a part-time docent at a historic house museum in his town thought to be a stop on the Underground Railroad. There he got to wear nineteenth-century garb and—after he'd studied letters in the house's archives—take on the role of the antislavery minister who had lived there in the mid-nineteenth century. Visitors enjoyed listening to him give his tours in character, speaking to them as if he was really an 1860s abolitionist.

While some of his fellow docents (part of his new community) thought Adam was a bit of a ham, they did encourage him to get involved with a local theater company. When I last saw him, he was involved with the annual holiday production of *A Christmas Carol*, in which, not surprisingly, he had been cast in the role of the gregarious Spirit of Christmas Present.

I attended the show, and I must say that when Adam made his appearance on stage in his long robe and fake beard and boomed Dickens's famous line "You have never seen the like of me before" to a quavering Ebenezer Scrooge, I couldn't help but think how true those words were. I had never seen Adam this happy, so in his element, so confident and obviously enjoying himself. While everyone in the audience of that community theater that night knew that Scrooge was about to be redeemed, I reveled in Adam's transformation. After many challenging years, he, too, was now flourishing.

Adam's climb from the perspectives to the pathways was a more arduous one than Sandi's. But it eventually got him to the same place.

The long stop in the mezzanine did the trick.

Self-Reflection

You may by now have a clear idea of what your goals are, and I hope some of the examples we've looked at have helped get your own creative juices flowing. And of course, I'm not talking about the inner artist that may or may not be in you. I just mean taking a creative look at the possibilities for you along the pathway, much as Adam and Sandi did.

Regardless, it's a good idea at this point to write down those goals. Before you do, though, go back and review the self-reflections you came up with during the perspectives stage.

My Case History

While it is important that we have goals and plans for how to proceed at the second level, one never knows where these pathways will lead, when they will intersect, or who might show up as a traveling companion.

In earlier chapters, I've shared with you my experience with postpartum depression. I'd like to share with you how I navigated the pathways once I had been treated for my depression—and how I ended up taking a very different route from what I had thought I would take as I traveled along the community pathway.

As a new parent, I had heard about the Waldorf schools, also known as Steiner schools in recognition of their founder, Rudolf Steiner. Although the schools are secular, they are steeped in Christian symbolism and rituals, which include seasonal celebrations based in the Christian liturgical calendar such as Michaelmas and Martinmas. This fresh encounter with Christianity—followed by the deaths of both of my parents in their early sixties from cancer—renewed my interest in religion. I also explored the Quaker faith via their Seekers program and began attending the local Unitarian church. I appreciated the mysticism of Steiner's beliefs, the social activism of the Quaker community, and the Unitarian commitment to inclusivity and to "deeds over creeds." But I was looking for something more.

Enter Doug. He was the patient of a colleague who had invited him to sit in on a Hopkins symposium that I was also attending. A bit of a character, I noticed him in a straw boater hat sitting alone at the lunch break, enjoying his complimentary catered meal of a sandwich and chips. I asked if I could join him.

"Are you really just after my chips?" he said with a twinkle in his eye.

I laughed, we started talking, and in some ways, the dialogue has continued since that very moment. Doug told me he was a historian by training and a former dean of a small liberal arts college in the Midwest. He was a fascinating conversationalist, and soon I found myself with a new friend. I later met his wife, Nancy, and they met my husband. The four of us became good, supportive friends. We talked about everything, even such "taboo" subjects as sex, politics, and religion, a topic in which Doug was particularly well informed as, I learned, he was a member of a parish run by the Society of Jesus, an order founded by St. Ignatius and associated with education since its beginnings.

About a year after meeting these new friends—punctuated by a visit to the transcendent Sistine Chapel in Rome—Jorge Mario Bergoglio was chosen to be the new pope of the Roman Catholic Church, taking Francis as his papal name in honor of Saint Francis of Assisi. I had never taken any notice of the papal enclave process; I didn't even know what "white smoke" meant. Pope Francis certainly grabbed my attention, in part because he was from Latin America (an area of interest from my undergraduate days) and in part because he was a Jesuit, as I had developed an interest in the Jesuits owing to my new friends. In fact, he was the first Jesuit pope in the history of the Roman Catholic Church.

And thus, I resumed my faith journey. I knew next to nothing about Catholicism and had never attended a Catholic service. As I started reading about the religion, however, I found that it encompassed the aspects I most admired of the other faiths I had dabbled in. There were rituals that followed the liturgical calendar and social teachings that emphasize the interconnectedness among all human beings, whether they are rich and strong or weak and poor. I was also drawn to the fact that Catholicism played a prominent role in the history and development of Western civilization and continues to be practiced internationally by over a billion people.

When I expressed interest in attending a Catholic service, Doug and Nancy welcomed me to their Jesuit parish. I ended up enrolling in the Rite of Christian Initiation of Adults (RCIA), a weekly, year-long process by which prospective converts are gradually introduced to aspects of Catholic beliefs and practices. I had been baptized in a Presbyterian church as a child, so did not have to be baptized again, but at that year's Easter service, I was confirmed and received first communion in the Roman Catholic Church.

Some of my friends that were raised Catholic—and who had participated in this rite of passage, familiar to any Catholic family, in which large groups of little boys in suits and girls in dresses receive their first communion en masse—thought this was pretty funny.

"I was six years old when I received first communion!" one of my friends chuckled. "Are you going to be standing there with all the first graders?"

Indeed, I realize I am a very different kind of Catholic. A born-again Catholic, if you will. I also know that my new religion may not be for everyone. But it has given me hope even in the most difficult and challenging of situations, including my brother's suicide, and brought me to a deeper understanding of my purpose in life. There are of course other communities in which I have sought meaning—the arts community, for example, which has provided such a wonderful pathway for many of my patients. But I realized, from my self-examinations in the perspectives stage of my own recovery, that the church offered me particular things that I found attractive and comforting.

For example, regular participation is demanded (I am highly conscientious and so very much like the idea of being accountable). A great emphasis is put on ritual and beauty (I love the stained glass at my local church, the communion chalices, the elaborate ecclesiastical robes), and the Jesuits have a long tradition of intellectualism (appealing to someone who works at a university and has always considered herself intellectually curious).

My becoming a Catholic was as surprising to me as it was to some of my friends and family. But it wasn't an impetuous decision. Doug entered the script of my life at just the right moment. At that point, I had done my homework: I had looked at and considered the perspectives of my own life, and had paused on the mezzanine to set some long-term goals, before ascending to the upper level. And so I was ready to take this particular route when he and Nancy became part of my life, and I was confident in my decision.

Catholicism has become a cherished part of my life, providing, quite unexpectedly, the community pathway that has enabled me to flourish.

chapter 9

Thriving in Your Best Life

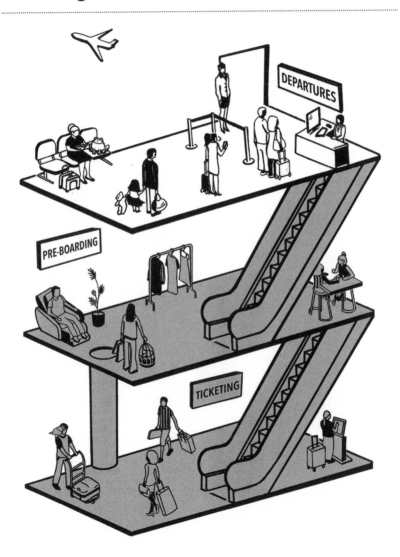

Each of us chooses the kind of life we want to live. It is critical to our dignity as human beings to retain the freedom to make our own decisions in these matters. Even if I disagree with choices that my patients make, as long as an illness is not infringing on their free will, I believe strongly in their right to decide how they want to live their own lives.

Even though my patients choose different paths, one thing most of them have in common is that they don't want their lives defined by a mental illness. They want to get back in the driver's seat. They want to get back to a life where they can feel satisfied, fulfilled, and happy in whatever they do.

In other words, they want to flourish.

In these pages, I have offered my story and others from among my patients to illustrate to you a model that enables those with mental health challenges to achieve that goal—despite the travails and stigma of a mental illness that they may have endured.

As you have read, the perspectives/pathway approach worked for me, it worked for many of my patients, and it can work for you.

In the last chapter, I showed you how to make the transition from the perspectives to the pathway, how to set goals and create your road map. If you stick with it, you will soon see yourself advancing along these routes.

Maybe like Jessica, the animal-loving patient of mine who overcame her agoraphobia and became a trainer of service dogs, you might find a job that suits your special talents (on the work pathway). Maybe like Zack, who once he had gotten his obsessive-compulsive disorder under control reengaged with his childhood passion of fishing and found a whole new community of fellow anglers that enriched his life, perhaps you will find community in a shared interest or belief. Maybe like Sandi, the successful woman who was depressed and unhappy with her life, you will be able to establish yourself on the family pathway by coming up with new ways to enjoy old relationships—as she and her husband did with ballroom dancing. Maybe like Paul, who was hospitalized at one time because of his schizophrenia, you will advance on all four pathways and make your strides on the education pathway by taking a psychology class!

Or maybe like me, you will find a new joy in family and a new community through faith.

I offer my story as a way of providing an example of the four common pathways to flourishing and to spark reflection in you about the importance of these pathways—family, education, work, community—in your life and that of your loved ones. These are the pathways that will lead to happiness, physical and mental well-being, a sense of meaning and purpose, strength of character, and close social relationships. These are the pathways that will lead to wellness and allow you or your loved one to flourish despite mental illness.

But based on my patients' and my own experience I also want to provide some cautionary words.

You cannot attempt to flourish and resolve a mental illness simultaneously. While the premise of this book is that those with mental illness can flourish, you cannot move onto the pathways until you are out of the acute stage of your illness—that is, until you have undergone the treatment and, if needed, taken the medications necessary to ensure that you are past the active phase of addiction, your depression, or whatever psychiatric illness you may have had. That needs to come first.

Flourishing takes time. Few people are born into a life of effortless ascendancy, but those who have had to deal with a mental illness have an added burden. While I have seen some patients with very serious illnesses make positive changes in their lives with remarkable speed, and while very often, one positive change can lead to another, reaching an optimal state rarely happens overnight. We all proceed down the pathways at variable speeds. There may be a few dead ends, and there are likely to be a few steps backward. But as with most other things in life, if you stick with it, if you continue to seek, say, a new community of friends or faith, to rebuild old family ties, to seek out opportunities, formal or informal, to learn, and so forth, you will eventually succeed. The various aspects of life that you bring together will eventually lead you to the life you envision.

It's not always smooth sailing, once you get there. At the risk of stating the obvious, nobody is fully happy, fully satisfied in every aspect of their lives all of the time. I believe that I can honestly say that in general,

I am flourishing in my life now more than ever—but that doesn't mean I don't have frustrations or that I never have days when I feel discouraged or doubt my abilities. We all do. And we all want to be a little better tomorrow than we are today.

Very often, external events can create roadblocks on our pathways. The tragic death of my brother, which I related to you earlier, shook me deeply—as such a tragic event would most people. I can honestly say that I was *not* flourishing after his suicide. However, as I also noted, it was not long after that that I became involved with my new faith community. This buoyed me at a time when I was very down, and it continues to sustain me today. Indeed, despite the loss of my brother, my participation in organized religion ended up getting me to a much better place than I had been before (although of course I wish he were here to see that).

Your trajectory toward thriving, toward flourishing, will likely have similar bumps. Change is hard. Setbacks are expected. Fear, discouragement, exhaustion, failures, adversity—these are all expected. But don't give up. They are all part of the pathway to success, not indications of failure. Rest assured that as you proceed along the pathways, taking the small steps needed in each area, you will get there.

How does it feel to flourish? How do you know when you've arrived? And is this a final destination—or more of an ongoing process?

Flourishing is not necessarily about material success. Even though the term "flourishing" is often used as a synonym for "growth" and "profitability," as in "a flourishing business," and while I am not naive enough to think that money is not important, one's net worth does not correlate with one's level of flourishing. We all know miserable millionaires. The case of my patient Sandi illustrates this: she was very successful and she was very unhappy. While I understand that people need to be able to pay their bills and put a roof over their head and I realize that the security of having a few bucks in the bank for that proverbial rainy day can reduce a lot of anxiety, dollar signs do not equate with flourishing.

As for me, although I'm no longer languishing in the throes of a depression, suffering from ennui owing to feeling a lack of meaning in my life, or bereaving my brother's death as deeply as I did in the first days and months after he died, and even though I am flourishing, I've not yet reached my final destination. None of us has. Nor would we want to. Flourishing is an active state of trying to be a little better today than we were yesterday, to live a little more fully, to love a little more deeply, to give a little more freely. Active flourishing may also mean taking on a more tangible goal: to eat more healthily, to exercise more vigorously, or—in my case—to sing a little more in tune. (I'd always wanted to be able to belt out a tune, and so I've been practicing at local karaoke nights!)

Film director Tim Burton once said that "anyone with artistic ambitions is always trying to reconnect with the way they saw things as a child." I think this applies to all of us, whether one has artistic ambitions or not. I know it applies to me. I've talked already about how my conversion to Catholicism has been such a positive change in my life. In the past few years, I've also reached several other landmark destinations on my pathways. One of them was an opportunity to reflect and reconnect with a part of myself that had been long dormant during my career in medicine. I'd studied the visual arts in college, and so when the chance to get in on the ground floor of an emerging field in medicine— art museum–based medical education—came up last year, I was all in. I completed a fellowship at the Harvard Macy Institute and am now working with educators at the Baltimore Museum of Art to help medical students flourish as physicians and human beings. This is going to help doctors use the arts as a way to explore what it means to be human, to be a physician, and to lead a good life (whether one is a patient or a clinician). In the process, I'm reconnecting with my first love—visual arts— and flourishing as well.

And I've continued to try and advance along my family pathway— quite literally. My husband and I have gotten in the habit of taking a one-hour walk together every morning. Our destination? A local Starbucks, so we get our workout and, yes, our caffeine, too—and just as importantly it's time where we can connect. Also, every Sunday afternoon, we get together as a family—along with Clay, now twenty-eight—to watch football, have a meal, and enjoy each other's company.

That's where I'm at on my flourishing journey. Wherever you are on that same quest—in the acute stage of a mental illness, in the early phases of recovery, beginning to feel like yourself again, or starting to feel like you're flourishing—the important thing is that *you* are in the pilot's seat. As William Ernest Henley wrote in his memorable poem "Invictus": "I am the master of my fate/I am the captain of my soul." You are, as well. So, I urge you to take the pilot's seat, and go forward in your life. With the help of friends, family, and community, may you soar, may you fly—may you flourish!

resources

Crisis

National Suicide Prevention Lifeline: call 1-800-273-8255 or visit https://suicidepreventionlifeline.org (24/7).

Suicide hotlines by state: visit http://www.suicide.org/suicide-hotlines.html to find resources for your state.

National Alliance on Mental Illness: call 1-800-950-NAMI (6264), Monday through Friday 10 a.m.–6 p.m. ET, or email info@nami.org.

Crisis Text Line: text HOME to 741741 for support (24/7) or visit https://www.crisistextline.org.

National Domestic Violence Hotline: call 1-800-799-7233 or chat online at https://www.thehotline.org (24/7).

National Sexual Assault Hotline: call 1-800-656-4673 or chat online at https://hotline.rainn.org/online (24/7).

Veteran Crisis Line (serves all veterans, service members, national guard, and reserve as well as family members and friends): call 1-800-273-8255 and press 1 or chat online at https://www.veteranscrisisline.net/; or text 838255. Deaf or hard of hearing: call 1-800-799-4889 (24/7).

International suicide hotlines: visit http://www.suicide.org/international-suicide-hotlines.html to find resources for your country.

General

American Foundation for Suicide Prevention: visit https://afsp.org/find-support and https://afsp.org/about-suicide.

Substance Abuse and Mental Health Services Administration (SAMHSA):

visit https://www.samhsa.gov and https://findtreatment.gov or call
1-800-662-4357.
SAMHSA Behavioral Health Treatment Services Locator: visit https://
findtreatment.samhsa.gov.
National Institute on Drug Abuse: visit https://www.drugabuse.gov,
https://www.drugabuse.gov/drugs-abuse, and https://www.drugabuse
.gov/publications.
National Institute of Mental Health: visit https://www.nimh.nih.gov,
https://www.nimh.nih.gov/health/topics/index.shtml, and https://www
.nimh.nih.gov/health/find-help/index.shtml.
National Alliance on Mental Illness: visit https://www.nami.org, https://
www.nami.org/Learn-More, and https://www.nami.org/Find-Support.
Ask Hopkins Psychiatry: visit http://askhopkinspsychiatry.org/q-a.
Mental Health America: visit https://www.mhanational.org/finding-therapy.
Mentalhealth.gov: visit https://www.mentalhealth.gov.
National Network of Depression Centers: visit https://nndc.org and
https://nndc.org/resource-links.
American Psychiatric Association: visit https://www.psychiatry.org
/patients-families.
Human Flourishing Program at the Institute for Quantitative Social Science:
visit https://hfh.fas.harvard.edu/measuring-flourishing and https://hfh
.fas.harvard.edu/how-to-flourish.

references

Introduction. Rise and Shine!

Holtyn, A. F., F. Toegel, S. Subramaniam, B. P. Jarvis, J. M. Leoutsakos, M. Fingerhood, and K. Silverman. 2020. Abstinence-contingent wage supplements to promote drug abstinence and employment: A randomised controlled trial. *Journal of Epidemiology and Community Health* 75 (5): 445–52.

Kachan, D., L. E. Fleming, S. Christ, P. Muennig, G. Prado, S. L. Tannenbaum, X. Yang, et al. 2015. Health status of older US workers and nonworkers, National Health Interview Survey, 1997–2011. *Preventing Chronic Disease* 12 (9): e162.

McHugh, P. R., and P. R. Slavney. 1998. *The perspectives of psychiatry.* 2nd ed. Johns Hopkins University Press.

McKee-Ryan, F., Z. Song, C. R. Wanberg, and A. J. Kinicki. 2005. Psychological and physical well-being during unemployment: A meta-analytic study. *Journal of Applied Psychology* 90 (1): 53–76.

Paul, K. I., and K. Moser. 2009. Unemployment impairs mental health: Meta-analyses. *Journal of Vocational Behavior* 74 (3): 264–82.

VanderWeele, T. J. 2017. On the promotion of human flourishing. *Proceedings of the National Academy of Sciences* 114 (31): 8148–56.

VanderWeele, T. J., E. McNeely, and H. K. Koh. 2019. Reimagining health—flourishing. *JAMA* 321 (17): 1667–68.

van Rijn, R. M., B. E. Carlier, M. Schuring, and A. Burdorf. 2016. Work as treatment? The effectiveness of re-employment programmes for unemployed persons with severe mental health problems on health and quality of life: A systematic review and meta-analysis. *Occupational and Environmental Medicine* 73 (4): 275–79.

Chapter 1. Are You Flourishing?

Collier, L. 2016. Growth after trauma. *Monitor on Psychology* 47 (10): 48. http://www.apa.org/monitor/2016/11/growth-trauma.

Dickens, C. 1868. *The adventures of Oliver Twist*. Ticknor and Fields.

Frankl, V. E. 1985. *Man's search for meaning*. Simon and Schuster.

National Opinion Research Center. General Social Survey. https://gss.norc.org.

Pennington, J. 2015. A biblical theology of human flourishing. Institute for Faith, Work, and Economics. https://tifwe.org/wp-content/uploads/2015/03/A-Biblical-Theology-of-Human-Flourishing-Pennington.pdf.

Seligman, M. E. 2012. *Flourish: A visionary new understanding of happiness and well-being*. Simon and Schuster.

Tedeschi, R. G., and L. G. Calhoun. 1996. The posttraumatic growth inventory: Measuring the positive legacy of trauma. *Journal of Traumatic Stress* 9 (3): 455–71.

VanderWeele, T. J. 2017. On the promotion of human flourishing. *Proceedings of the National Academy of Sciences* 14 (31): 8148–56.

VanderWeele, T. J., E. McNeely, and H. K. Koh. 2019. Reimagining health—flourishing. JAMA 321 (17): 1667–68.

Chapter 2. A New Vision for Understanding Mental Illness

American Psychiatric Association. 2013. *Diagnostic and statistical manual of mental disorders*, 5th ed. American Psychiatric Association.

Chisolm, M. S., and C. G. Lyketsos. 2012. *Systematic psychiatric evaluation: A step-by-step guide to applying "the perspectives of psychiatry."* Johns Hopkins University Press.

Costa, P. T., Jr., and R. R. McCrae. 1992. *Professional manual: Revised NEO Personality Inventory (NEO-PI-R) and NEO Five-Factor Inventory (NEO-FFI)*. Psychological Assessment Resources.

Engel, G. L. 1980. The clinical application of the biopsychosocial model. *American Journal of Psychiatry* 137 (5): 535–44.

Ghaemi, Nassir. 2015. Martin Luther King's manic-depressive illness: A source of his greatness and despair. *Medscape Psychiatry*, October 26.

Jamison, K. R. 1996. *Touched with fire*. Simon and Schuster.

Jamison, K. R. 2015. *An unquiet mind*. Picador.

Jamison, K. R., and T. A. Traill. 2017. *Robert Lowell, setting the river on fire: A study of genius, mania, and character.* Knopf.

McHugh, P. R., and P. R. Slavney. 1998. *The perspectives of psychiatry.* 2nd ed. Johns Hopkins University Press.

Saks, E. R. 2007. *The center cannot hold: My journey through madness.* Hachette UK.

VanderWeele, T. J. 2017. On the promotion of human flourishing. *Proceedings of the National Academy of Sciences* 114 (31): 8148–56.

Chapter 3. The First Step on Your Journey

McAdams, D. P. 2011. Narrative identity. In *Handbook of identity theory and research,* ed. S. J. Schwartz, K. Luyckx, and V. L. Vignoles, 99–115. Springer Science + Business Media.

Chapter 4. The Importance of Personality Types

Costa, P. T., Jr., and R. R. McCrae. 1992. *Professional manual: Revised NEO Personality Inventory (NEO-PI-R) and NEO Five-Factor Inventory (NEO-FFI).* Psychological Assessment Resources.

McHugh, P. R., and P. R. Slavney. 1998. *The perspectives of psychiatry.* 2nd ed. Johns Hopkins University Press.

Saklofske, D. H., and M. R. Schoenberg. 2011. Wechsler Adult Intelligence Scale (all versions). In *Encyclopedia of clinical neuropsychology,* ed. J. S. Kreutzer, J. DeLuca, B. Caplan, 2675–80. Springer.

Chapter 5. The Role of Habits in Your Behavior

McLeod, S. A. 2007. Skinner: Operant conditioning. Simply Psychology. http://www.simplypsychology.org/operant-conditioning.html

McLeod, S. A. 2014. Bobo doll experiment. Simply Psychology. https://www.simplypsychology.org/bobo-doll.html.

McLeod, S. A. 2017. Behaviorist approach. Simply Psychology. https://www.simplypsychology.org/behaviorism.html.

Richter, C. P. 1922. A behavioristic study of the activity of the rat. *Comparative Psychology Monographs* 1 (2): 1–55.

Chapter 6. Mental Illness as a Disease

Harvard Medical School. 2007. National Comorbidity Survey, table 1: Lifetime prevalence DSM-IV/WMH-CIDI disorders by sex and cohort. https://hcp.med.harvard.edu/ncs/ftpdir/NCS-R_Lifetime_Prevalence _Estimates.pdf.

Perälä, J., J. Suvisaari, S. I. Saarni, K. Kuoppasalmi, E. Isometsä, S. Pirkola, T. Partonen et al. 2007. Lifetime prevalence of psychotic and bipolar I disorders in a general population. *Archives of General Psychiatry* 64 (1): 19–28.

Schultz, S. G. 2002. William Harvey and the circulation of the blood: The birth of a scientific revolution and modern physiology. *Physiology* 17 (5): 175–80.

Chapter 7. The Four Pathways to Fulfillment

Amato, P., and J. Sobolewski. 2001. The effects of divorce and marital discord on adult children's psychological well-being. *American Sociological Review* 66 (6): 900–921.

Balbuena L., M. Baetz, and R. Bowen. 2013. Religious attendance, spirituality, and major depression in Canada: A 14-year follow-up study. *Canadian Journal of Psychiatry* 58 (4): 225–32.

Call, V. R. A., and T. B. Heaton. 1997. Religious influence on marital stability. *Journal for the Scientific Study of Religion* 36 (3): 382–92.

Chida, Y., A. Steptoe, and L. H. Powell. 2009. Religiosity/spirituality and mortality: A systematic quantitative review. *Psychotherapy and Psychosomatics* 78 (2): 81–90.

Cuñado, J., and F. P. de Gracia. 2012. Does education affect happiness? Evidence for Spain. *Social Indicators Research* 108 (1): 185–96.

Gallup. Religion. https://news.gallup.com/poll/1690/religion.aspx.

Gangadharan, L., and P. Maitra. 2003. The effect of education on the timing of marriage and first birth in Pakistan. *Journal of Quantitative Economics* 1 (1): 114–33.

Kaplan, R. M., and R. G. Kronick. 2006. Marital status and longevity in the United States population. *Journal of Epidemiology and Community Health* 60 (9): 760–65.

Kim, H. K., and P. C. McKenry. 2016. The relationship between marriage and psychological well-being: A longitudinal analysis. *Journal of Family Issues* 23 (8): 885–911.

Koenig, H. G., D. E. King, and V. B. Carson. 2012. *Handbook of religion and health*. 2nd ed. Oxford University Press.

Krause, N., and R. D. Hayward. 2012. Religion, meaning in life, and change in physical functioning during late adulthood. *Journal of Adult Development* 19 (3): 158–69.

Kreager, D. A., R. B. Felson, C. Warner, and M. R. Wenger. 2013. Women's education, marital violence, and divorce: A social exchange perspective. *Journal of Marriage and the Family* 75 (3): 565–81.

Lambert, N. M., F. Fincham, S. R. Braithwaite, S. Graham, and S. Beach. 2009. Can prayer increase gratitude? *Psychology of Religion and Spirituality* 1 (3): 39–49.

Lambert, N. M., F. D. Fincham, D. C. Lavallee, and C. W. Brantley. 2012. Praying together and staying together: Couple prayer and trust. *Psychology of Religion and Spirituality* 4 (1): 1–9.

Lambert, N. M., F. D. Fincham, T. F. Stillman, S. M. Graham, and S. R. Beach. 2010. Motivating change in relationships: Can prayer increase forgiveness? *Psychological Science* 21 (1): 126–32.

Li, S., O. I. Okereke, S.-C. Chang, I. Kawachi, and T. J. VanderWeele. 2016. Religious service attendance and lower depression among women— A prospective cohort study. *Annals of Behavioral Medicine* 50 (6): 876–84.

Lim, C., and R. D. Putnam. 2010. Religion, social networks, and life satisfaction. *American Sociological Review* 75 (6): 914–33.

Lochner, L. 2011. *Non-production benefits of education: Crime, health, and good citizenship*. NBER Working Paper 16722. National Bureau of Economic Research. www.nber.org/papers/w16722.

Lochner, L., and E. Moretti. 2004. The effect of education on crime: Evidence from prison inmates, arrests, and self-reports. *American Economic Review* 94 (1): 155–89.

Maier, E. H., and M. E. Lachman. 2000. Consequences of early parental loss and separation for health and well-being in midlife. *International Journal of Behavioral Development* 24 (2): 183–89.

Mamun, A. A. 2008. *Effects of employment on marriage: Evidence from a randomized study of the Job Corps Program*. Final Report. Mathematica Policy Research Center.

Marks, N. F., and J. D. Lambert. 1998. Marital status continuity and change among young and midlife adults: Longitudinal effects on psychological well-being. *Journal of Family Issues* 19 (6): 652–86.

McKee-Ryan, F., Z. Song, C. R. Wanberg, and A. J. Kinicki. 2005. Psychological and physical well-being during unemployment: A meta-analytic study. *Journal of Applied Psychology* 90 (1): 53–76.

Musick, M. A., J. S. House, and D. R. Williams. 2004. Attendance at religious services and mortality in a national sample. *Journal of Health and Social Behavior* 45 (2): 198–213.

Paul, K. I., and K. Moser. 2009. Unemployment impairs mental health: Meta-analyses. *Journal of Vocational Behavior* 74 (3): 264–82.

Pew Research Center. 2012. *The global religious landscape*. Pew-Templeton Global Religious Futures Project. https://assets.pewresearch.org/wp -content/uploads/sites/11/2014/01/global-religion-full.pdf.

Pew Research Center. 2014. Record Share of Americans Have Never Married. *Social and Demographic Trends*, September 24. www.pewsocialtrends .org/2014/09/24/record-share-of-americanshave-never-married/.

Powdthavee, N., W. N. Lekfuangfu, and M. Wooden. 2015. What's the good of education on our overall quality of life? A simultaneous equation model of education and life satisfaction for Australia. *Journal of Behavioral and Experimental Economics* 54: 10–21.

Putnam, R. D., and D. E. Campbell. 2012. *American grace*. Simon and Schuster.

Ryff, C. D., and S. M. Heidrich. 1997. Experience and well-being: Explorations on domains of life and how they matter. *International Journal of Behavioral Development* 20 (2): 193–206.

Sayer, L. C., P. England, P. D. Allison, and N. Kangas. 2011. She left, he left: How employment and satisfaction affect women's and men's decisions to leave marriages. *AJS: American Journal of Sociology* 116 (6): 1982–2018.

Shariff, A. F., A. K. Willard, T. Andersen, and A. Norenzayan. 2016. Religious priming: A meta-analysis with a focus on prosociality. *Personality and Social Psychology Review* 20 (1): 27–48.

Shor, E., D. J. Roelfs, P. Bugyi, and J. E. Schwartz. 2012. Meta-analysis of marital dissolution and mortality: Reevaluating the intersection of gender and age. *Social Science and Medicine* 75 (1): 46–59.

Strawbridge, W. J., S. J. Shema, R. D. Cohen, and G. A. Kaplan. 2001. Religious attendance increases survival by improving and maintaining good health behaviors, mental health, and social relationships. *Annals of Behavioral Medicine* 23 (1): 68–74.

Stutzer, A., and B. S. Frey. 2006. Does marriage make people happy, or do happy people get married? *Journal of Socio-Economics* 35 (2): 326–47.

Sweeney, M. M. 2002. Two decades of family change: The shifting economic foundations of marriage. *American Sociological Review* 67 (1): 132–47.

Uecker, J. E. 2012. Marriage and mental health among young adults. *Journal of Health and Social Behavior* 53 (1): 67–83.

VanderWeele, T. J. 2017. Religion and health: A synthesis. In *Spirituality and religion within the culture of medicine: From evidence to practice*, ed. M. J. Balboni and J. R. Peteet, 357–402. Oxford University Press.

VanderWeele, T. J., S. Li, A. C. Tsai, and I. Kawachi. 2016. Association between religious service attendance and lower suicide rates among US women. *JAMA Psychiatry* 73 (8): 845–51.

VanderWeele, T. J., J. Yu, Y. C. Cozier, L. Wise, M. A. Argentieri, L. Rosenberg, J. R. Palmer, et al. 2017. Attendance at religious services, prayer, religious coping, and religious-spiritual identity as predictors of all-cause mortality in the Black Women's Health Study. *American Journal of Epidemiology* 185 (7): 515–22.

Wilcox, W. B., and N. H. Wolfinger. 2016. *Soul mates: Religion, sex, love, and marriage among African Americans and Latinos*. Oxford University Press.

Wilson, C. M., and A. J. Oswald. 2005. *How does marriage affect physical and psychological health? A survey of the longitudinal evidence*. IZA Bonn Discussion Paper 1619. Institute for the Study of Labor.

Wood, R. G., B. Goesling, and S. Avellar. 2007. *The effects of marriage on health: A synthesis of recent research evidence*. Mathematica Policy Research.

Chapter 8. Your Road Map to Go from Surviving to Thriving

Henley, W. E. Invictus. 1919. In *The Oxford book of English verse*, ed. A. T. Quiller-Couch. Clarendon.

Mandolesi, L., A. Polverino, A. Montuori, F. Foti, G. Ferraioli, P. Sorrentino, and G. Sorrentino. 2018. Effects of physical exercise on cognitive functioning and wellbeing: Biological and psychological benefits. *Frontiers in Psychology* 9: art. 509.

acknowledgments

....

In anticipation of writing this, I spent a solitary morning taking in the vivid personal visions of the artists whose works are displayed at Baltimore's American Visionary Art Museum. These artists are individuals who, for the most part, have had no formal art training and have faced extraordinary life challenges, both internal and external. They've struggled with addiction and other psychiatric illness, neglect, abuse, homelessness, incarceration, racism, and even genocide. These works, through which each artist shares personal visions of their world with us, are often startling and sometimes disturbing, but the intensity of the artist's drive to create meaning and even joy from adversity is always palpable, and instructive. I am continually moved by the power, utility, and sheer necessity of art in the human experience.

Although this book is born of my personal experiences with psychiatric illness, my own life has been mostly free of the challenges that these artists and my patients have confronted on a daily basis. This is a matter of unearned fortune, nothing more. So, my first acknowledgment for this book is to God, for the blessings of a life relatively free of suffering but also for the personal hardships I have faced, without which I would not be as valuable a doctor to my patients or teacher to my students. It is from my sufferings—my brother's suicide, my own depression—that I've learned much about being a good physician, and for that I am grateful.

The second acknowledgment is to my patients who—through sharing their own personal hopes, dreams, fears, challenges, losses, and achievements with me—have given my life a deeper sense of meaning and purpose. Thanks to each of them I am a better person and clinician. I also

want to thank my supportive family—especially my husband and son—
for bearing the sacrifices that come with having a wife and mother who is
a physician, and a neurotic one at that. They both have an extraordinary
sense of humor. They would have to.

This book wouldn't have been possible without the editorial team at
Johns Hopkins University Press. Thanks especially to Barbara Kline Pope,
Greg Britton, and Joe Rusko for believing in this project enough to introduce me to John Hanc, who agreed to cowrite this book with me. We
shared many laughs over cultural touchstones from our day (Does "'You
rang?' ring a bell?) and drowned our sorrows together when the Ravens
football team didn't quite advance to the Super Bowl. John is the best!

I also want to thank Margot Kelly-Hedrick, my amazing mentee and
research assistant, who read many drafts of the manuscript and who
fact-checked all of the references and compiled the resources for patients
and family members. Margot is now a medical student at Duke University, well on the road to being one of the best clinicians, teachers, and researchers the world has ever known. It was an absolute joy working with
Margot on this project and others.

Special thanks to Natasha Chugh, an extremely talented illustrator,
who is currently an undergraduate student at Johns Hopkins University.
Natasha and I have worked on numerous publications together, but none
required as many illustrations as this project. Many thanks to Natasha for
translating some pretty complex psychiatric concepts into images that are
at once accessible, serious, and upbeat (and Natasha's beautiful cover im-
age perfectly captures this tone as well).

Of course, this book owes a huge debt to the work of Tyler Vander-
Weele, a leader in drawing causal links from large epidemiologic data
sets. His studies on flourishing provide the scientific evidence on which
I base my teaching enterprise, which ultimately is focused on the importance of getting to know our patients as people in order to improve health
care outcomes. Science in collaboration with the arts and humanities can
illuminate certain truths about what it means to be human, to be a health
care professional, and to lead a good life (for clinicians and their patients).
This is now my life's work: bringing together these lessons from science
and the arts and humanities to enrich the education of health professions
learners. Thanks to Tyler for doing such impeccable research so that I can
spend my time in the art museum teaching medical students how to be
better doctors!

And, finally, I want to thank a few of the giants on whose shoulders I stand. I would be nothing without my teachers and mentors, many of whom are within the Department of Psychiatry at Johns Hopkins led by Dr. James Potash. I want to start by thanking Dr. Phillip Slavney, my residency program director; he taught me how to evaluate patients in a way that is both empathic and systematic, a method from which thoughtful and personalized treatment plans emerge. His dedication to rigorous, "nonflabby" thinking about psychiatric illness has benefited generations of psychiatrists and their patients. He, along with the late Dr. Jerome Frank (one of my long-term psychotherapy supervisors), taught me how important the patient-doctor relationship is to healing illnesses of all kinds, knowledge I continue to pass down to my students and residents. Thanks to Dr. Slavney for never failing me!

I also want to thank Dr. Kostas Lyketsos, with whom I trained and now work. He recruited me out of private practice in 2006 to join the full-time faculty at Johns Hopkins and provided the mentorship that allowed me to carve out my own unique path as a clinician educator. Thanks to Kostas, who has been by my side since the beginning of our careers at Hopkins, including when we were chief residents. He believed in me when few did, and I am honored to be his friend and colleague. And I would be remiss if I didn't acknowledge the mentorship of Dr. Catherine D. DeAngelis, who was the first woman editor in chief of JAMA, the American Medical Association's journal (2000 to 2011). She has been a friend and mentor, helping me with the professional development challenges faced by women in academic medicine. Thanks to Dr. De!

Finally, I want to thank Dr. Paul McHugh, one of the leading intellectuals of our time whose knowledge of both the sciences and the humanities is vast. Whether I have a question about Abraham Lincoln or William James or William Shakespeare, I can always turn to him for the answer. He knows more about poetry than I ever will, and he is always generous in his teaching. Dr. McHugh's mission in life is to be a part of the times in which he lives, a mission he has certainly succeeded in! Nothing makes him happier than a lively exchange of ideas. And whether I agree with his ideas or not, engaging in discussions with Dr. McHugh always sharpens my thinking. I am grateful for all that he has taught me about medicine, art, literature, psychiatry, leadership, and life. Thanks to Dr. McHugh, to whom I will be forever indebted.

index

consequences in behavior perspective, 47–48

creativity, mental illness linked with, 29

cues in behavior perspective, 48

David, Larry, 38

dementia, 53

depression: case study, 118–20; community pathway and, 104; disease perspective, 90–91, 94; life story perspective, 68; postpartum depression, 78–79, 85, 94

Diagnostic and Statistical Manual of Mental Disorders (DSM), 30–31, 44, 61–62, 85

Dickens, Charles, 16

dimensional perspective: defined, 4; for mental illness, 37–47; personality and, 79; potential in, 44, 47; provocation in, 44–45, 47, 76–77; response in, 45, 47; self-reflection, 46–47

disease perspective, 88–95; author's case history, 94–95; defined, 4; depression and, 90–91, 94; etiology, 52–53, 88, 89, 91; for mental illness, 52–55, 88–95; pathophysiologic process, 52–53, 98, 90, 91–92; self-reflection, 54, 93–94; syndrome, 52–53, 54, 88–89, 91

divorce, 102, 104

drives in behavior perspective, 48–49, 51, 81–82

drug use. *See* substance use

eating disorders: anorexia nervosa, 49, 54, 88, 116; bulimia, 109

education pathway to flourishing, 7, 9–11, 17, 101–2

Engel, George, 30

etiology of disease, 52–53, 98, 90, 92

eudaimonia, 16

evidence-based research, 12

extraversion, 39, 72, 73–76, 79

extrinsic rewards, 48

faith communities, 103–4, 110, 122–25

family pathway to flourishing, 7, 9–11, 17, 97–99

fatigue, 57, 59–60, 68, 70

financial and material security domain, 9, 19

flourishing: case study, 20–25; defining, 15–20; domains of, 19; formula for, 106–7; PERMA model of, 16; self-reflection, 26–27. *See also* pathways to flourishing

Francis (pope), 123

Frankl, Victor, 19

free association, 62

Freud, Sigmund, 82

genetic mutation, 53

goal-directed actions, 81

grief, 32–33, 88

habits, 80–87. *See also* behavior perspective

happiness and life satisfaction domain: behavior perspective and, 50; defining, 19; dimensional perspective and, 44–45; life story perspective and, 59, 68, 70; mental illness and, 28–29; pathways to flourishing and, 97, 98, 101, 128

Harvard Macy Institute, 130

Harvey, William, 91

Hemingway, Ernest, 29

Henley, William Ernest, 123

HIDE acronym, 5–6, 56, 88, 113

homicide, 48

Huntington disease, 53

imagination, 40

impulse control, 43, 85, 87

innate drives, 48, 81–82

introversion, 39, 72, 73–75, 79

IQ, 73, 77

Jamison, Kay, 29
Jesuits, 123
Johns Hopkins: author's residency
  training at, 66; behavior studies at,
  82–83; Center for Addiction and
  Pregnancy, 87; holistic approach, 16–
  17, 55, 91; perspectives of psychiatry
  approach to mental illness, 30, 31;
  Weight Management Center, 84

Kafka, Franz, 29
King, Martin Luther, Jr., 28–29

learning in behavior perspective, 47–48,
  81–83
life satisfaction. *See* happiness and life
  satisfaction domain
life story perspective, 57–71; author's
  case history, 57–58, 64–69; defined,
  4; detailed history, 59–60; for mental
  illness, 32–36; mental status examination, 59–60, 62–63; multiple sources
  of information, 62; observations
  before interpretations, 63; outcome,
  35–36; self-reflection, 34–36, 70–71;
  sequence, 35–36; setting, 35–36

maladaptive behavior, 44, 83
manic-depressive illness, 29, 65
marriage, 97, 102
McAdams, Dan, 69
meaning and purpose domain, 19
mental illness, 28–56; author's case
  history, 93–94; behavior perspective, 47–50; dimensional perspective,
  37–47; disease perspective, 52–55,
  89–94; life story perspective, 32–36;
  self-reflection, 34–36, 46–47, 50–51,
  55, 93–94
mental status evaluation, 59–60, 62–63,
  74
Meyer, Adolf, 16–17, 60
mood changes, 54

narratives: life story perspective and,
  69; rescripting of, 33–34, 70–71
NEO-PI (Neuroticism, Extraversion,
  Openness Personality Inventory), 74,
  77, 78
neuroticism, 38, 72, 74, 75, 79
New York University, 66
Nimoy, Leonard, 38

obsessive-compulsive disorder (OCD),
  107–9
openness, 40
operant conditioning, 82
outcome for life story perspective,
  35–36

pathophysiologic process of disease,
  52–53, 88, 90, 91–92
pathways to flourishing, 7–12, 17, 96–
  111; case studies, 107–11; community pathway, 7, 9–11, 17, 103–5; education pathway, 7, 9–11, 17, 101–2;
  family pathway, 7, 9–11, 17, 97–99;
  formula for flourishing and, 106–7;
  happiness and, 97, 98, 101, 128;
  work pathway, 7, 9–12, 17, 100–101
Pavlov, Ivan, 82
Pennington, Jonathan, 16
PERMA model of flourishing, 16
personality dimensions, 72–79; antisocial personality disorder, 88; author's case history, 78–79; dimensions of, 38–44; life story perspective
  and, 58; premorbid personality, 74;
  self-reflection, 77
perspectives of psychiatry approach to
  mental illness, 30, 31, 108, 116
Plath, Sylvia, 29
postpartum depression, 78–79, 85, 94
posttraumatic growth, 19
potential in dimensional perspective,
  44, 47
premorbid personality, 74

provocation in dimensional perspective, 44–45, 47, 77

Quakers, 123
Quinto, Zachary, 38

religious communities, 103–4, 110, 123–25
rescripting, 33–34, 70–71
resilience, 77
response in dimensional perspective, 44, 47
rewards in behavior perspective, 48–49, 52
Richter, Curt, 83
Ripken, Cal, Jr., ix–xi
roadmap for flourishing, 7–12, 112–25; author's case history, 122–25; case studies, 118–21; preboarding, 115–16; ready for takeoff, 117–18; self-reflection, 122

Saks, Elyn: *The Center Cannot Hold*, 29
schizophrenia, 29, 88; case study, 20–25
self-reflections: behavior perspective, 51–52, 84–87; community pathway to flourishing, 105; dimensional perspective, 46–47; disease perspective, 55, 93–94; flourishing, 26–27; life story perspective, 34–36, 70–71; mental illness, 34–36, 46–47, 51–52, 55, 93–94; personality dimensions, 77; roadmap for flourishing, 122; work pathway to flourishing, 100–101
Seligman, Martin, 16
sequence for life story perspective, 35–36, 58
setting for life story perspective, 35–36
Skinner, B. F., 82
socially shaped drives, 83–84
social relationships. *See* close social

relationships domain; community pathway to flourishing; education pathway to flourishing; family pathway to flourishing; work pathway to flourishing
Steiner, Rudolf, 123
Stevenson, Bryan, 102
stigma, 78–79, 93–94, 127
substance use: behavior perspective, 80–81, 85–87; dimensional perspective, 77; life story perspective, 65, 67; pathways to flourishing and, 109–161 roadmap for flourishing and, 120–21
suicide, 48, 67, 87
suprachiasmatic nucleus, 83
syndrome in disease perspective, 52–53, 54, 88–89, 91

Tedeschi, Richard, 19, 20
temperament, 38–44, 77. *See also* personality dimensions
trauma, growth after, 19
True Justice (documentary), 102

University of Maryland, 66

VanderWeele, Tyler J., 17, 19, 26–27, 28
Van Gogh, Vincent, 29
virtue. *See* character and virtue domain
vitamin B12 deficiency, 53
volunteer work, 11, 104–5, 115

Waldorf schools, 123
Watson, John B., 82
Wechsler Adult Intelligence Scale (WAIS), 73
work pathway to flourishing, 7, 9–12, 17, 100–101

·